THE WAY TO HAPPINESS

The Eternal Quest of Mankind

By ALFRED ARMAND MONTAPERT

HERE ARE THE NOBLEST AND FINEST IDEAS OF
THE WORLD'S GREATEST MEN ON HAPPINESS.
FORMULAS TO A BETTER AND HAPPIER LIFE.

PRENTICE-HALL, INC.   ENGLEWOOD CLIFFS, N.J.

ADDITIONAL COPIES MAY BE ORDERED FROM

BOOKS OF VALUE
2458 Chislehurst Drive
Los Angeles, CA 90027

Books by the Same Author

DISTILLED WISDOM
Thoughts that Successful Men Live By

SUPREME PHILOSOPHY OF MAN
The Laws of Life

PERSONAL PLANNING MANUAL
How to Increase Your Worth

© 1978, by

Alfred Armand Montapert

All rights reserved, no part of this book may be reproduced in any form or by any means, without permission in writing from the publisher.

Second Printing July 1978

Library of Congress Cataloging in Publication Data
Montapert, Alfred Armand.
　The way to happiness.
　1. Happiness. 2. Success. I. Title.
BF575.H27M66　　158'.1　　77-13678
ISBN 0-13-946228-7

PRENTICE-HALL, INC., ENGLEWOOD CLIFFS, NEW JERSEY
PRINTED IN THE UNITED STATES OF AMERICA

TABLE OF CONTENTS

Happiness: The Eternal Quest Of Mankind	6
The Ingredients For Happiness	8
Happiness Comes From Within	10
Thinking Happy Thoughts	12
Kindness Is An Element Of Happiness	14
Giving And Serving Others	16
Appreciate Your Possessions	18
Enjoy Your Work	20
Happiness Is A Habit	22
Happiness Depends Upon You	24
Worthwhile Values	26
True And False Pleasures	28
The Quest For Joy	30
The Love Of God Brings Joy	32
The Way We Meet The Events Of Life	34
Sorrow And Suffering	36
Hope Is An Element Of Happiness	38
Formula For Happiness	40
Enjoy The Beauty Of Nature	42
The Results Of A Happy Life	44
Character Influences Happiness	46
Moods And Their Influence	48
Cheerfulness	54

Table of Contents

I Would Grow In Grace And Strength ... 55
Faith or Frenzy ... 56
Beneficial Inactivity ... 57
Chasing Rainbows ... 58
Ten Steps To Brighten Your Life ... 59
Today ... 60
Appreciation ... 61
Things For Which I Am Glad ... 62
Real Wealth ... 63
Right Words Bring Happiness ... 64
Happiness Is A Vacation ... 68
An Active Mind Can Keep You Young ... 71
Happiness Reduces Stress ... 72
God's Happy World ... 75
True Education Brings Joy ... 76
The Happy Choice ... 81
The Natural Laws Of Life ... 84
Friendship Brings Happiness ... 86
Friendship ... 87
What Do You Want From Life? ... 88
I Heard A Happy Bird Note ... 92
A Happy Present ... 94
The Happy Magic Trail ... 96
A Happy Life ... 99

Table of Contents

Contentment..100
The Happiness Of Spring..............................102
Seeking Happiness 104
Growth..106
Credo..107
Think Happy Noble Thoughts 108
Love Is Supreme Happiness 110
Silence Fosters Happiness 112
Differences In People 114
Balance In Living...116
Prayer Brings Joy..118
Loyalty Is An Element Of Happiness 119
How Does One Know Himself? 120
I Wonder..124
Go Into The Fields......................................125
The Simple Happy Life...............................126
Today's Investment—Tomorrow's Dividend..................130
Happiness Is A Brook 132
The Country Is A Happy Place 133
Happiness Depends On Planned Action....134
Man's Most Happy Goal..............................136
Good Philosophy For Happiness 137
The School Of Life......................................138
Summary 141

HAPPINESS: THE ETERNAL QUEST OF MANKIND

THE MOST IMPORTANT THING TO LEARN IN LIFE IS HOW TO LIVE. Happiness is many different things. Few people are aware how many elements go into making the product happiness.

MAKE UP YOUR MIND TO BE HAPPY. Learn to find happiness in simple things. When the famous French writer, Colette, was dying of cancer and was being interviewed by a newsman, she exclaimed, "*What a wonderful life I've had! Those were my happiest days!*" Then after a sigh of remorse she added, "*I only wish I'd realized it sooner.*"

Our biggest mistake in our pursuit of happiness is not knowing when we have it. THE MOST IMPORTANT PRODUCT OF OUR LIFE IS HAPPINESS AND JOY. The fountain of happiness is in the heart. HAPPINESS IS WHEN YOU FEEL GOOD INSIDE. Make this your chief goal—to spend your life experiencing happiness and joy.

The capacity to enjoy life is inborn in all living beings, but JOY, like LIFE, does not sustain itself. It must be cultivated. The noxious weeds of worry and strife, rush and rumpus, must be constantly rooted out. Each of us must be the gardener who labors together with God, if the finest things of life are to come to full flower and fruit. BE HAPPY—FEEL GOOD—ENJOY LIFE!

THE WAY TO HAPPINESS PROMISES MUCH. It will perform still more. It will be a delightful adventure filled with the flowers of experience, and above all, with the smiles of happy people. According to Goethe, *"Man's worth, as well as his happiness, depends upon his ability to give value to his existence."*

THE QUESTS OF LIFE are many and varied. Among them are the Quest of MONEY, and POSSESSIONS, the Quest of LOVE, the Quest of TRUTH, the Quest of USEFULNESS and DUTY, the Quest of GOODNESS and of God; and the Quest of HAPPINESS and CONTENTMENT.

All of us were born a long way from ourselves, and the climb to reach ourselves is a long steep climb. Treadmill complacency will never get us to the top. If we are content to creep, we shall never grow wings for flying. Mere drifters soon became deadwood on the slow sluggish current of indifference. Man reaches his full potential by constantly seeking practical real-life wisdom for his Happiness and life.

The uncertain conditions, and the insecurity in a rapidly changing world, are one of the chief causes of unhappiness. By contrast, according to Aristotle and others, HAPPINESS IS THE QUALITY OF A WHOLE LIFE. It is not attained through self-gratification, but through fidelity to a worthy purpose, which provides the anchor we need in a sea of uncertainty.

If it were possible to measure on a meter the happiness of the life a person leads, or the quality of life, we might be shocked by how much we are shortchanging ourselves. Are you low or high on the Happiness Scale? The quality one develops in one's life style has a profound influence on health, wealth and happiness.

THE INGREDIENTS FOR HAPPINESS

It takes the grinding of 57 facets to get the maximum brilliance from a diamond. So it is with happiness. There are many facets, or ingredients, which contribute to happiness. The elements are all in this book and the results can be miraculous!

The chief ingredients of happiness are the right spirit and wholesome employment. Few people realize how much of their happiness is dependent upon their work. *True happiness comes from giving of ourselves for a purpose.* Live CONSTRUCTIVELY and live OPTIMISTICALLY. Do the BEST you can, EACH DAY.

Coleridge writes: *"The happiness of life is made up of minute fractions, the little, soon forgotten charities of a kiss, a smile, a kind look, a heartfelt compliment, and countless other infinitesimals of pleasant thought and feeling."*

HAPPINESS IS A SPIRITUAL QUALITY. HAPPINESS IS FOUND IN A MULTITUDE OF LITTLE THINGS—a mind full of rich thoughts, a heart full of compassion, kindness, serving others, helping others, forgetting about self, keeping active, creative effort, achievement, seeing and appreciating the beauty of nature, the song of a bird, a sunrise or a sunset, friends and a family to share life's beauty with you, *the ability to enjoy the good things that are here.*

The Ingredients for Happiness

Victor Hugo remarked, *"What I really value is neither fame, fortune, nor genius, but loving and being loved."*

True happiness is a by-product of successful living. Many things make up true happiness—health, attitude, something to love, something to do, something to hope for, faith, truth, kindness, aptitude, laughter, achievement. Much happiness is overlooked because it doesn't cost anything. MORE HAPPINESS IS TO BE GAINED BY SELF-DENIAL THAN BY SELF-INDULGENCE.

Gelett Burgess says, *"Laughter is a real medicine. It has optimistic vitamins in it. It revives like oxygen. It restores failing morale. I have proved for myself the cleansing power of laughter."*

There are two levels of happiness, and the human heart is designed to live on both. One level is MUNDANE HAPPINESS. The other is DIVINE HAPPINESS. Mundane happiness grows thin and quickly loses its glow. Genuine happiness, or JOY, has its source in God and is the Summum Bonum or Supreme Good. It will never lose its luster. St. Augustine said, *"We are made for God and will be dissatisfied until we have God in our hearts."* Man might possess everything tangible in the world and yet not be happy, for happiness is the satisfying of the soul.

Happy living can be attained by the right organization of personal effort, and the right selection of one's life work and environment. It flows from the development of one's Spiritual Dimension, and genuine love and heart union with your mate. Love is not to be declared, or uttered, or spoken, but shall be revealed by deeds. Love is demonstration, not declaration. Happiness is being married to the one you love.

HAPPINESS COMES FROM WITHIN

I cannot emphasize too strongly that we must NOT LOOK OUTSIDE for our happiness, BUT IN OURSELVES, in our own heart and mind. We keep on looking for happiness to come to us from without, from other people, from things, or from time itself.

To find happiness we must search our hearts, our own beliefs and efforts. We must have the AWARENESS of beauty, joy, goodness, love. *Keep your heart free from hate, your mind from worry . . . live simply . . . expect little . . . give much.*

HAPPINESS DEPENDS MUCH MORE ON WHAT IS WITHIN THAN WITHOUT US. Happiness is an aptitude. To be happy is not the purpose of our being, but to DESERVE HAPPINESS. Be kind. Remember everyone you meet is fighting a hard battle.

"Neither wealth nor rank will ensure happiness," says John Lubbock. *"Without love and charity and peace of mind, you may be rich and great and powerful, but you cannot be happy."* Smile, brighten up your life, help yourself feel cheerful and happy. Begin the day with some pleasant, inspiring music. Be more optimistic, tell yourself: *"Today will be a good day, I will make it better than yesterday."*

Happiness comes from within; it is the revelation of the depths of the inner life—just as light and heat reveal the sun from which they radiate. Each man is the creator of his own happiness; it is the aroma of a life lived in harmony with high ideals. *Joyous people are not only the happiest, but the longest lived, the most useful and the most successful. BE HAPPY—FEEL GOOD.*

The Constitution of America only guarantees pursuit of happiness. *The man who is truly happy is he who enjoys a serenity of soul, the causes of which flow from his inner life.* The more profound this inner life is, the loftier the motives which direct it, the more beautiful, intense, and permanent will be the happiness which it produces. This would be a happier world if happiness were a status symbol.

In happiness there is an element of self-forgetfulness. When you are happy you lose yourself in something outside yourself. The opposite is also true. When you are desperately miserable, you are intensely conscious of yourself and become a solid lump of ego weighing a ton. People get into ruts and don't realize what they are doing. They actually blame the cause of their own trouble on others.

FORGET GOING OUT AND CONQUERING THE WORLD, GO IN AND CONQUER YOURSELF! Then you will have mastered the universe within you. Men are going to learn sometime that this inner world of man is very much bigger than we have ever suspected. We are going to realize that the INNER MAN, the real you of you . . . the heart, the mind, the soul, spirit, is a UNIVERSE in itself.

W. Beran Wolfe writes, *"The cultivation of laughter and a sense of humor is excellent training for the good life. There is no better method of establishing a bond between yourself and your fellowmen than to cultivate a genial and humorous personality. Only those who feel reasonably safe and successful can afford to laugh."*

THINKING HAPPY THOUGHTS

"The happiness of your life," said Marcus Aurelius, *"depends upon the character of your thoughts."* Mind rules the body, and our thoughts are power releases for good or bad. The mind is our invisible control center. Happiness starts here just as a spring is the start of the river. OUR MIND PRODUCES FOR US RESULTS ACCORDING TO OUR BELIEF.

If health and happiness are to be ours we must learn to MASTER OUR THOUGHTS. We set the mood of each day by our attitudes and thoughts. If we indulge in negative, resentful, unkind or impure thinking we become tense, unhappy, depressed, fear-ridden individuals. If we fill our minds with what is positive, worthy and beautiful, we gradually build integrated, poised, power filled lives. Health and genuine happiness depend on positive thinking and faith in God.

Humor is a spice to living. It adds flavor to work, zest to play, charm to self-improvement, and proves to others that we have a security within ourselves. Will Rogers remarked, *"We are all here for a spell, get all the good laughs you can."*

Every good thought contributes its share to the ultimate result of your life. A single thought in the morning may fill the whole day with joy and sunshine, or with gloom or depression. Many a day has been dampened by a careless or unkind thought. *You will never be any better or higher than your best thoughts.* "This is the day the Lord hath made; let us rejoice and be glad in it."

That the mind has great power over the body there is not the slightest doubt. To consciously think that "I CAN" impels the subconscious faculties into action. Life is formed from the inside out. WHAT I AM INSIDE DETERMINES THE ISSUES IN THE BATTLE OF LIFE. Motives are invisible but they are the true test of character.

Our personal body chemistry is guided and triggered by our emotions but THOUGHT LEADS the emotions. You can make yourself sick, poor, and unhappy by your habitual thinking. You can even kill yourself by your thoughts. Dr. Gene Emmet Clark calls negative thoughts *"the world's most communicable disease."* Always remember, <u>the only person who can hurt you is YOU!</u> Thoughts of joy and happiness, and all that is good, are constructive.

Count your blessings, your real assets will always outweigh your liabilities. Don't feel afraid of anything as you travel through life. Feel confident and full of faith as you climb the hills of life. This is God's world and it belongs to all of us who claim its abundance, so make yourself at home and be very happy. Whatever man's outward circumstances, inner serenity and happiness can be acquired, at least gradually, by anyone. When a person makes statements of fear, doubt, unbelief, etc., the pilot light to destruction is lit.

The happiness of your life depends upon the quality of your thoughts. Thinking is only a process of talking to oneself intelligently. You talk to yourself all the time, be careful what you say. All rewards in this life are for right thinking and acting. If we think right we will act right, THE MIND RULES THE BODY. UNHAPPINESS IS A WASTE OF ONE'S OWN LIFE, AND A BURDEN TO SOCIETY.

KINDNESS IS AN ELEMENT OF HAPPINESS

Guard within yourself the treasures of happiness which come from kind words, kind acts, kind looks, warm handshakes—these are all ACTS OF KINDNESS. *Lead the life that will make you a kindly and friendly person to everyone around you, and you will be surprised what a happy life you will live.*

To cultivate kindness is a valuable part of the business of living. When talking to people always remember to be KIND . . . COMPASSIONATE . . . THOUGHTFUL . . . UNDERSTANDING . . . LOVING AND HAPPY. I have always been sorry and felt bad after every occasion when conditions or events made me angry. When you are mad or irritated you can't think properly. You are tense and under stress and strain. *When you are happy you are RELAXED and CALM and your thoughts flow freely.* It is difficult to tell how much our minds are comforted by a kind manner and gentle speech. *SMILE AND FEEL GOOD.*

SMILING IS AN ART. Many think they know how to smile. In a true smile the eyes also smile. *A SMILE IS A THING TO ENJOY.* The best salesmen, the best actors, the most successful leaders of people know that smiles will get you where money can't—a lot of times.

A laugh, to be joyous, must flow from a joyous heart, and without kindness there can be no true joy. The older you get the more you realize that kindness is synonymous with happiness.

Kindness Is An Element of Happiness

Our former neighbor, Aldous Huxley, in speaking before a general audience, made this statement: *"It is a little embarrassing that after forty-five years of research and study, the best advice I can give to people is to be a little kinder to each other."*

It's not great deeds that make people's lives happy, it is the little kindnesses of daily life. *Kindness is the oil that takes the friction out of life.* The opportunities are countless each day for bestowing a kind word, rather than a bitter, sarcastic one. Three of the greatest expressions to use as you travel through life are: "Thank you," "I am sorry," . . . "I love you."

"Stop complaining about the management of the universe," says Henry Van Dyke. *"Look around for a place to sow a few seeds of happiness."* THE PERSON WHO SOWS SEEDS OF HAPPINESS REAPS A CONTINUAL HARVEST. Happiness can't be preserved for future use—you just have to keep planting new seeds each day.

THE BENEFITS OF BEING HAPPY ARE MANY. If you are a sales person, on your next call, see how happy you can be and notice how much easier your negotiation turns out. Your thoughts flow freer when you are happy and not tense. Your happy attitude is contagious and spills over onto others around you. When you laugh you relax, and when you relax you give freedom to muscles, nerves and brain cells. Man seldom has use of his reason when his brain is tense. The sense of humor makes a relaxed condition where reason can act. Or, just suppose you have to work with a difficult person, see how happy you can be, and you will be amazed how well you get along with him. *The RESULTS from being happy are SO GREAT, I can't understand why anyone would want to be unhappy.*

GIVING AND SERVING OTHERS

Half the world is on the wrong track in the pursuit of happiness. They think it consists in HAVING AND GETTING and in BEING SERVED by others. Happiness consists in GIVING and SERVING others. Happiness is a thing to be practiced daily like a violin.

Each of us must make the little circle in which we live better and happier. Be able to say, *"I have made one human being at least a little wiser, or a little happier, or at least a little better this day."* Mark Twain wrote: *"To get the full value of a Joy, you must have somebody to divide it with."*

"Happiness is a perfume," said Emerson, *"which you can't pour on someone without getting some on yourself."* Men are rich only as they give. Action and reaction are always equal. Give largely and receive largely—whether it be money, service, friendship, faith or confidence.

When you plant a seed, you expect a crop. YOUR GOOD DEEDS ARE YOUR SEED. It is a Natural Law . . . You reap what you sow, good or bad. *"Let us not be discouraged in well-doing for in due season ye shall reap,"* says the Bible.

Some people forget you never GET a dividend unless you MAKE AN INVESTMENT. This applies to the financial, physical, mental, spiritual and social realms. You will find enjoyment in serving others. It will add zest to your life, and YOUR HAPPINESS WILL INCREASE DAILY.

Edwin Markham wrote, *"There is a destiny that makes us brothers, none goes his way alone; all that we send into the lives of others, comes back into our own."* You have to "give to get," this is a natural law. You have to put the logs into the fireplace before you can get the heat. It's as simple as that. Most people say, "When I get, then I will give." This is like putting the cart before the horse. WHAT I AM WORTH IS WHAT I AM DOING FOR OTHER PEOPLE.

Unless we think of others and do something for them we miss one of the greatest sources of happiness. Getters generally don't get happiness, givers get it. You simply give to others a bit of yourself . . . a thoughtful act, a word of appreciation, a lift over a rough spot, a sense of understanding, a timely suggestion. Unhappiness is the hunger to GET . . . happiness is the hunger to GIVE.

The happiest people I have known are those consumed with the desire to radiate happiness, to live unselfishly, to do everything within their power to help others. *Happiness is a by-product of an effort to make someone else happy.* Is anybody happier because you passed this way? Dr. Albert Schweitzer said, *"You will always have happiness if you seek and find how to serve others."* It has been well said that, *"Service is the rent we pay for our place on earth."* That kind of service brings the true happiness we all seek. HAPPINESS IS THE ONLY PRODUCT IN THE WORLD THAT MULTIPLIES BY DIVISION.

For what a man HAS, he may be dependent on others. What he IS, rests with him alone. What he OBTAINS in life is but acquisition; what he BECOMES is growth.

We long to leave something behind us which shall last, some influence or good that will outlive us. No one has ever been honored for what he received. HONOR . . . REAL HONOR . . . is reserved for what one GIVES!

APPRECIATE YOUR POSSESSIONS

Perhaps the dominant force in the average life is possessions. Life becomes a mad scramble for gain instead of a mission for God. *We are so busy making a living that we forget to make a life.* Life never gives all you want, be content with what you have. So . . . stick a daisy in your hat and be happy.

Cultivate fine taste and discrimination in your choice of things. Get a right idea of values. Material possessions that you do not need and cannot use may be only an encumbrance. Let your guiding rule be not how much but how good. A thing you do not want is dear at any price. Have a regular time for examination and elimination. Assimilate as you accumulate. Choose things that express your own individuality. Look for quality rather than for quantity. Have an occasional stocktaking and eliminate unsparingly.

Happiness does not depend upon wealth, position or possessions. *The happiest life is that which constantly exercises and educates what is best in us.* Man might possess everything tangible in the world and yet not be happy, for HAPPINESS IS THE SATISFYING OF THE SOUL. It is in the hands of the individual, and not in the hands of others. Success and happiness in life do not depend on our circumstances, but on ourselves, and HAPPINESS IS EQUALLY ACCESSIBLE TO ALL MANKIND.

"Few things are needful to make the wise man happy, but nothing satisfies the fool—and this is the reason why so many of mankind are miserable."—Francois de La Rochefocauld

Real happiness is not dependent on external things. In our frantic search for happiness we assume it resides in something that we can possess or manipulate—a special home, smart clothes, powerful automobiles or a huge bank account, expensive vacations or costly amusements. We are surely mistaken. If we do have material comforts and at the same time possess happiness, it means that our happiness stems from within ourselves. IT RESIDES IN WHAT WE ARE, not in what we have. ALL WE TAKE WITH US WHEN WE LEAVE THIS PLACE IS WHAT WE ARE.

Happiness does not come from possessions, but from OUR APPRECIATION of them. It does not come from our work, but from OUR ATTITUDE toward that work. It does not come from success, but from the SPIRITUAL GROWTH we attain in achieving that success. And the greatest adventure in our life is to learn the art of being happy. Live a more carefree life, get happiness out of the simple things of life. Don't follow the crowd, they will take you out into the woods and lose you. Cut down on exposures, don't let the world molest you.

What is the difference between POSSESSIONS and TREASURES? POSSESSIONS are outside of you. One can be loaded with possessions and empty inside, even miserable. TREASURES are inside of you. You feel the warmth and indwelling Presence of God in your life. *"Greater is He that is in you than he that is in the world."* GOD IS GREATER THAN ANY PROBLEM YOU HAVE, OR EVER WILL HAVE. God is the Greatest Power in the universe. There is a big difference between POSSESSIONS AND HEAVENLY TREASURES, and—like love—they cannot be defined but must be experienced. Every man's main objective in life is to really FEEL GOOD, TO ENJOY LIVING. Happiness is that which makes you FEEL GOOD INSIDE.

ENJOY YOUR WORK

Possibly the greatest source of human happiness is in personal achievement. "LEARN TO LIKE YOUR WORK" IS THE FIRST LAW OF SUCCESS AND HAPPINESS IN LIFE.

Find out what you can do best so that you may fulfill yourself in doing the work you have the greatest capacity to perform. When you are doing a worthwhile job, you receive satisfaction and joy from your work. You are happy, you feel good inside.

I have lived long enough to know that the secret of happiness is NEVER TO ALLOW YOUR ENERGIES TO STAGNATE. Happiness is the attribute of being completely and successfully active. To live the way you were designed to live. *"If a man is unhappy,"* wrote Epictetus, *"remember that his unhappiness is his own fault, for God made all men to be happy."*

All men desire three things: HEALTH, WEALTH, HAPPINESS. *"Happiness lies in the absorption in some vocation which satisfies the soul,"* writes Sir William Osler, the famous English doctor. Are you enjoying spending your life doing the things that give you the greatest happiness? Doing work that satisfies your soul? Giving value to your existence?

Thinking is the lightest work there is, but if you are tense and not relaxed it is hard mental work. Your mind will function better if you are relaxed and happy. The mind functions best when it is not driven or forced. EASY DOES IT!

Nature has everywhere written her protest against idleness; everything which ceases to struggle, which remains inactive, rapidly deteriorates. It is the struggle toward an ideal, the constant effort to reach higher and further, which develops manhood and character. *The secret of being happy is not in doing the things that make us happy, but in BEING HAPPY IN DOING THE THINGS WE HAVE TO DO.*

A wise father told his son: *"Nothing is ever accomplished without work. If I leave you nothing else but the will to work, I leave you the most priceless gift—the joy of work."* I wonder how many times lately you've used the word "Fun" in talking about your work? It's a pleasure to meet a man who seems to thoroughly enjoy what he is doing.

We live, eat, love, procreate, work. Why? Goethe answered: *"in order to raise as high as possible the pyramid of my existence, whose base was given to me ready-made."* A noble aim this, to try to make your life into a genuine, happy masterpiece. There is nothing like work to take your mind off your trouble. GET INTO A WORK THAT YOU LIKE. The money it pays should be secondary. The by-products of work are: HEALTH—HAPPINESS—STABILITY and CHARACTER. The day is approaching when we shall learn to estimate the importance of man, not by his income, but by his output. They call it PRODUCTIVITY.

How rapidly a man decays when he retires from active life! The unhappiest people on earth are those who have nothing worthwhile to occupy them. Congenial and useful work is the secret of mental and physical well-being. NO MAN, WOMAN OR CHILD CAN BE TRULY HAPPY UNTIL THEY HAVE SOME CONGENIAL WORK, SOME OCCUPATION IN WHICH THEY CAN PUT THEIR HEART, AND WHICH AFFORDS A COMPLETE OUTLET TO ALL THE FORCES WITHIN THEM.

HAPPINESS IS A HABIT

HAPPINESS IS A HABIT!—CULTIVATE IT! Happiness is a habit just as worry is a habit. The mind creates its pattern, then repeats the pattern over and over all day and all life long. The pattern can be constructive or destructive; the decision is yours to make every day: the time to be happy is NOW! It has often been said, *"What you are will determine what you do."* Not always. You may be much better than your worst act, and you may be much worse than your best act. What you HABITUALLY do is YOU.

WE LIVE LARGELY BY HABITS. L. G. Elliott writes, *"The long span of the bridge of your life is supported by countless cables called habits, attitudes, and desires. What you do in life depends how much you want it . . . how much you are willing to work and plan and cooperate and use your resources. The long span of the bridge of your life is supported by countless cables that you are spinning now, and that is why today is such an important day. Make the cables strong!"*

HAPPINESS DEPENDS NOT ON THINGS AROUND US, BUT ON OUR ATTITUDE. A life of earthly success is full of perils and anxieties. The habit of being happy enables one to be freed, or largely freed, from the domination of outward conditions. *If a man does not have the element of happiness within himself, not all of the beauty and variety, the pleasures and interests of the whole world can give it to him.* What a man IS contributes to his happiness more than what he HAS.

MAN IS A BUNDLE OF HABITS. Every single qualification for success is acquired through habit. Men form habits and habits form futures. If we do not deliberately form good habits, then we will unconsciously form bad ones. *YOU are the kind of person you are because you have formed the habit of being that kind of person—and the only way you can change for the better is through changing your habits.* The only real cure for a bad habit is to put a good habit in its place.

It is an established fact that SUCCESS IS A HABIT. FAILURE IS ALSO A HABIT. The important point is that man chooses his own pattern of thought. He makes his own blueprint for his future. He selects his own methods. MAN MAKES THE MAN. NO ONE ELSE DOES IT FOR HIM. HE DOES THE JOB HIMSELF. Man creates his own success, but he also creates his own failure. Success is not an accident. THE KEY IS TO ACQUIRE THE RIGHT HABITS. DEAL WITH YOUR BAD HABITS.

In life as we observe what others do, listen to what they say and read what has been written, ideas get through to us. Some of these we reject, and others we accept and attempt to carry out. Patterns of thinking and acting develop and become habits. Unlearning the wrong things is much harder to do than learning the proper things in the first place.

Silently and imperceptibly you are forming habits that will ultimately determine the degree of your happiness and success. Closely guard the QUALITY of your thoughts, that they may lead to RIGHT HABITS. *One of the secrets of happiness is found in the habitual emphasis of PLEASANT THINGS* and the persistent casting aside of all bad elements. Men make their own world! Sin and selfishness dig deep furrows in the face. CULTIVATE THE HAPPINESS HABIT!

HAPPINESS DEPENDS UPON YOU

"Every man ought to begin with himself, and make his own happiness first, from which the happiness of the whole world would at last unquestionably follow," wrote Goethe.

Happiness and contentment are not commodities which we import, neither do they depend upon "the abundance of things" which we possess. It is not WHERE WE ARE, WHAT WE HAVE, OR WHAT WE POSSESS that makes us happy or unhappy. WHAT WE ARE determines our state. A poor man can be immensely happy and a very rich man can be miserable. Happiness is a do-it-yourself condition. Happiness comes from emotional maturity. Balzac wrote, *"Happiness depends on what lies between the soles of your feet and the crown of your head."*

The most blessed kind of happiness is A STATE OF BASIC CONTENTMENT. Listen to the wise St. Paul: *"In whatever state I find myself, I have learned to be content."* Our goal should be: "ALWAYS BE CONTENT . . . with what we have, never with what we are." Sure, it's all right to aspire for things worthwhile, but everything that exceeds the bounds of moderation is destructive to a person's existence. And many things we do have no value.

Ella Wheeler Wilcox admonished: *"I'm going to be happy today, though the skies are cloudy and grey. No matter what comes my way, I'm going to be happy today."* Don't say, "Do we have any problems?" Say, "What are our problems?" I have to be personally in shape to meet them. I have to personally deal with myself. I am responsible for myself, for my resting, my eating, exercise, spiritual development, mental condition. The way you LIVE your life is your responsibility.

Be candid with yourself. Would you like to have a strong novelist like Dickens, or Hugo, or Balzac, describe you just as you are—your acts, words, thoughts, motives—turning the light on so that the whole world would know the exact truth about you? What changes would you like to make in the picture? Are you the kind of man you would like to see the world made of? If not, why not? What improvements must you make in yourself in order to win your approval and be the type of man you would be willing to see increase, and multiply, and occupy the earth? Be less critical, any fool can grumble. Smile more, don't take yourself so seriously. Enjoy every day, soon you will be smiling in your sleep.

Each passing day brings its peculiar burden and responsibility. From this warfare, to paraphrase Solomon, *there is no discharge.* Night and day one lives with the care and anxiety of it. On the other hand, EACH DAY BRINGS ITS JOY AND COMPENSATION.

John R. Heron, famous writer for the Royal Bank of Canada Newsletter, writes, *"There are five components of the happy life: health, work, interests, friendships, and the pursuit of an ideal. Get to know your qualities so as to enlarge them, and your failings so as to reduce them."*

YOUR HAPPINESS DEPENDS UPON YOU. Your mind is yours and can be used only by you. You must GOVERN YOUR OWN TONGUE. Your real life is your thoughts. Your thoughts are of your own making. Your character is your own handiwork. You must make your own decisions. You must abide by the consequence of your acts. You have to create your own ideas. You alone can regulate your habits. You must form your own ideals. You have to build your own monument . . . or dig your own pit. Which are you doing?

WORTHWHILE VALUES

According to a recent survey, people are happy only twenty percent of the time. Why? Because they have lost their conception of the true values of living. To be secure and happy, live in the values you want to experience.

Construct a moral ideal, for without it life will be devoid of satisfaction, and material gains will become dust and ashes. Develop self-respect by determining exactly what your values are, then having the self-discipline to stick by them at all times.

One of the great arts in living and happiness is to LEARN THE ART OF PRIORITY, and of ACCURATELY APPRAISING VALUES. We cannot safely tie to any material value. The value of all material possessions changes continually, sometimes overnight. Nothing of this nature has any permanent set value. The real values are those that stay by you, give you joy and happiness and enrich you. They are the human values.

Some of the true human values of life are: love, truth, character, happiness, attitude, honesty, discipline, kindness, health, loyalty, gratitude, prayer, creativity, conduct, responsibility, culture, balance, moderation, learning, development, a sense of God, action, human relations, survival, suffering, freedom, patience, achievement, spiritual development, moral fortitude, integrity, ethics, solid beliefs, self-esteem, mental health, leisure, confidence, confession, contentment, faith, hope, friendship, peace of mind.

Did you ever stop to think what would be the ideal life to live? Everyone should be given the opportunity to write it out, or give his expression. What are your PRINCIPLES and VALUES? These values are not only our first line of national defense, but they safeguard our character, our life and our fellowman. We cannot define God or any of the real values in life, yet they are the most stable things in our lives. These great values of life must be experienced. They produce worthy people.

WHEN YOU HAVE LOVE, HAPPINESS AND COMPANIONSHIP WITH YOUR MATE, YOU HAVE EVERYTHING. IT IS THE LOVE OF PEOPLE THAT IS VALUABLE, NOT THINGS. Even animals and birds have a deep love and dedication for their mates. Angels come to visit us and we only know them when they are gone.

Every day should be a happy day for thoughtful people. To be thankful to be alive and enjoy the real values of life, health, family and friendship. To see, enjoy, appreciate all the handiwork of nature. There is so much to live for and so much to do. It is our own fault if we do not enjoy life. *"All men,"* said Ruskin, *"may enjoy though few can achieve."*

In our generation, multitudes of people have had so much given to them and done for them, that THEY HAVE LOST THE GRATEFUL HEART. Each year we should be more joyful than ever before, because we have fewer years ahead in which to be joyful. *OUR CHIEF PRODUCT OF LIFE IS REALLY JOY.*

Our mad scramble for material things has become the bandit that has looted us clean of the wealth of goodness, and with the loss of genuine goodness has gone our greatness. We need a renewing of the sense of individual worth. THE TRUE VALUES!

TRUE AND FALSE PLEASURES

There is an essential difference between PLEASURE and HAPPINESS. Pleasure is temporary, transient, effervescent. We have it today . . . it's gone tomorrow. We spend weeks, months, or years in a feverish quest for it, only to find no lasting satisfaction or contentment.

"Think not to find thy happiness out there in the world of riotous pleasure," said Heinrich. *"Thy blessedness dwells in thine own breast, here thou must forever establish it."*

You are heir to the infinite glories, courage, virtues and wisdom of the past. You are heir, also, to the infinite shame, cowardice, vice and folly of the past. YOU have free choice. It is for you to choose which you will make your very own.

A man can reach as high as his ideals. Our happiness is fashioned according to our souls. By removing the millstones from around our neck and clearing the hurdles, our life can be a joyful experience.

Those who seek pleasure in "Wine . . . Women . . . and Song," or in a hundred frivolous and injurious ways, often find it leads to great unhappiness in the end. Flee the pleasure that bites tomorrow. In fact, our pleasures can lead to great unhappiness. Happiness is defined as *the pleasurable experience that springs from something good; contentedness.* Pleasure is defined as *an agreeable sensation or emotion, gratification, delight.*

"A life of indulgence, a 'gay life,' as it is falsely called, is a miserable mockery of happiness," admonished Lord Avebury. *"Those who have fallen victims to it, complain of the world, when they have only themselves to blame."*

True and False Pleasures

Why do people, in the name of pleasure, indulge in pastimes which must invariably lead to ill health and unhappiness? Should they not stop and think? Too many pleasures are like invading a wasp's nest . . . MORE STING THAN HONEY. Every EXCESS has its EFFECT, its AFTERMATH, its HANGOVER. Everything that exceeds the BOUNDS OF MODERATION has an UNSTABLE FOUNDATION.

The luxuries of Campania weakened Hannibal, whom neither snows nor Alps could vanquish; victorious in arms, he was conquered in pleasure.

To get an idea of our fellow countrymen's miseries, we have only to take a look at their pleasures. ALL PLEASURE MAY BE BOUGHT AT THE PRICE OF PAIN. The difference between false pleasure and true pleasure is just this: for the true, the price is paid before you enjoy it; for the false, after you enjoy it.

John Lubbock writes, *"The true pleasures are almost innumerable. Relations and friends, conversation, books, music, poetry, art, exercise, and rest. The beauty and variety of Nature, summer and winter, morning and evening, day and night, sunshine and storm, woods and fields, rivers, lakes and seas, animals and plants, trees and flowers, leaves and fruit, are but a few of them."*

A bell is not a bell until you ring it.
A song is not a song until you sing it.
Love in your heart is not put there to stay.
Love is not love until you give it away.

—*Oscar Hammerstein*

THE QUEST FOR JOY

Someone has said, *"All the world is seeking happiness."* Actually, all the world is in search of something infinitely deeper and more abiding than mere happiness. That something is JOY. JOY IS CONTENTMENT THAT FILLS THE SOUL, A STATE OF HEART.

Conrad Richter writes, *"The chief product of life, which modern planners mistakenly consider ease, is really JOY."* Joy is spiritual prosperity. That motto above your desk—"SMILE." How did that ever get into so many business offices? Try it. Joy makes the face shine, and he that has a merry heart has a continual feast.

The difference between happiness and joy is more than a mere play on words. *Joy is the abiding fellowship with God, which experiences no change amid the vicissitudes of life.* Happiness can be superficial, based on an abundance of things one possesses but which may evaporate. Joy is deep, abiding spiritual union with the unchanging God.

Pleasure or happiness are not the same as joy. A wicked and evil man may have pleasure, while any ordinary person is capable of being happy. Pleasure generally comes from things and always through the senses; happiness comes from humans through fellowship. Joy comes from loving God. Samuel Butler wrote: *"Man, unlike the animals, has never learned that the sole purpose of life is to enjoy life."*

God's formula for joy is: *"Say and do what is pleasing in the sight of the Lord. Trust and obey God's Word."* I believe the root of all happiness on this earth lies in the realization of a spiritual life with a consciousness of something wider than materialism; in the capacity to live in a world that makes you unselfish because you are not over-anxious about your personal place; that makes you tolerant because you realize your own human fallibilities; that gives tranquility without complacency because you believe in something so much larger than yourself.

"*A man's life,*" said Jesus Christ, "*is not fulfilled nor is it filled full of, nor by, the abundance of things which he possesses.*" Here is one of the most important statements ever given a bewildered, heart-hungry world. The shallowness and futility of superficial happiness is its dependence upon things—congenial companions, good clothes, a bank balance, a comfortable home. These things, of course, contribute to the sum of life, but the point is THEY ARE NOT THE FIRST NEEDS OF LIFE.

JOY IS A LIVING SPRING HIDDEN DEEP IN THE INNER LIFE THAT IS NOT DEPENDENT UPON THINGS. We live in a rough-and-tumble world. "*In the world,*" Christ said, "*Ye shall have tribulation,*" but He further added, "*Be of good cheer.*"

What is the practical value of seeking joy as well as happiness? JOY IS STRENGTH. An Old Testament writer said, "*The joy of the Lord is your strength.*" The joyful person will surpass all others in spiritual strength, poise, and usefulness. Joy is content, and contentment is the positive, constructive, creative force on which life depends for both health and happiness. JOY IS SPIRITUAL PROSPERITY. JOY MAKES YOU FEEL GOOD INSIDE.

Solomon said, "*There is no wealth greater than the health of the body, there is no joy greater than the joy of the heart . . . A cheerful heart causes man's life to blossom, while the spirit of sadness dries the bones. Never rejoice at other people's misfortunes for you cannot know when adversity may come to you.*"

THE LOVE OF GOD BRINGS JOY

THE HUMAN HEART IS NEVER SATISFIED. It seeks peace that only the love of God and the full acceptance of God can bring. In other words, ONLY GOD CAN SATISFY THE SOUL OF MAN. Only then is man complete, or whole, when he has his spiritual union with the Creator of life. And this belief, if genuine, makes a man ten times the man he formerly was!

Through God, your situation—no matter what you are going through—is not hopeless. Be a person with FAITH in God. If we choose exemption from life's battles, we leave no choice but to be exempted from the rewards of victory. TRUE PROSPERITY IS THE ABILITY AND KNOWLEDGE TO RECEIVE GOD'S POWER TO MEET ANY NEED—WHETHER IT BE PHYSICAL . . . MENTAL . . . SPIRITUAL . . . FINANCIAL . . . OR SOCIAL. FAITH IS THE NAME OF GOD'S CREATIVE POWER.

The secret of happy days is not in our outward circumstances, but in our own hearts. *"The Kingdom of Heaven is within you."* The Kingdom indicates a dominion and God is our King, and we are citizens of the Kingdom, and God dwells in our heart. When this condition takes place in man, a real joy flows out from his heart like a spring. This is the only permanent way to have peace of soul that wells up in joy, contentment and happiness. And the only security for happiness is to have mind and heart filled with the love of the Infinite and Eternal.

Success and happiness hinge on the capacity to believe, on an abiding faith in a Higher Power. *HAVING A SENSE OF*

GOD is not only YOUR REAL SECURITY, but also one of the most rewarding of all human achievements—THE ART OF REAL HAPPINESS.

The failure of man to make a happy world in which God's gifts are shared and man lives happily with man, is in man himself. The power man needs is the love which is released when he is in living touch with God. The unpardonable sin is to shut God out of your life. It is not so much your comprehension of God as it is your spiritual development that counts.

In the heart of every person there is a HUNGER, a longing for something that you cannot find in this world. It is the soul that longs for a comforting spirit, a fellowship with God, the Supreme Power. Apart from God, man exists, but does not live. Apart from God and His Word, man only guesses and theorizes and gropes and stumbles along in the blindness of his own finite understanding.

A great and wise man has well said, *"It is absolutely essential that I know God."* Essential because time will pass, things will perish, human relationships will cease and the brightest prospects of our most exciting hopes will become black and barren. Nor do we need better evidence of this truth than the fact that we so soon outgrow the *"delights that thrill our little selves."* *To experience the Infinite is my one hope of finding the inexhaustible God, and God alone is* THE ANSWER TO THE INFINITE DEMANDS OF THE INFINITE ME OF ME.

Let shallow minds reject and ridicule as they may, the fact remains that God's truth is at the center of all education in living, for there is no explanation of the universe, nor of man, apart from the creative genius of God.

THE WAY WE MEET
THE EVENTS OF LIFE

"*I am more and more convinced that our happiness or unhappiness depends far more on the way we meet the events of life,*" Humboldt admonishes, "*than on the nature of those events themselves.*" Nothing in life is STATIC; one must LEARN to make adjustments.

N. W. Hillis writes, "*Life is for growth, all events are educational, and all work toward culture and refinement. It follows, then, that trouble and adversity are among the chosen teachers. However, Happiness is latent in every form of trouble and suffering. If the soul was built for happiness, then happiness must be possible, despite trouble and sorrow.*"

Victory over events . . . There is no station so low, no occupation so humble, no neighborhood so bad, no temptation so severe, but that the soul may ride victorious over its misfortune. Reality is not the way you wish things to be. Not the way they appear to be. BUT THE WAY THEY ACTUALLY ARE. TO BE HAPPY WE MUST FACE REALITY.

When Channing, the great scholar, orator, and author, became incapacitated by physical affliction, he said, "*It is forbidden me to speak or write, but not to aspire and be. I shall live content with small means; to seek elegance rather than luxury; refinement not fashion; to be worthy not rich. I shall think quietly, act bravely, await occasions, and never hurry.*" By perfecting himself, man obtains more and more mastery over events.

LIFE IS NOT DATED MERELY BY YEARS. EVENTS ARE SOMETIMES THE BEST CALENDARS.

We say of almost any crisis hour, *"These are the times that try man's soul."* Well, my observation is just ordinary everyday living is the severest test of all. There are always times in life when things don't go the way you want. The fellow who keeps steadily on his way, contented and happy, when there is no unusual stress of circumstances to force the issue, is a hero indeed.

Reverses that no one could have anticipated overtake the man, and the fortune of a lifetime melts like the dissolving snow; enemies arise to undermine reputation, the skies rain abusive and cruel lies; soon happiness is poisoned at its very spring. Circumstances change suddenly and one is often caught by surprise. Adversity must be reckoned with as we reckon with gravity.

Plato said, *"Conflict is noble, and hope is sublime."* So let us enter upon a battle for our happiness, a battle that is now more necessary than ever. Voltaire wrote, *"Life is a battle,"* and he wasn't kidding. Events crowd into everyone's life, but their outcome depends entirely upon the individual. Fanny Crosby wrote, *"I am the happiest soul living. If I had not been deprived of my sight, I would never have received so good an education, nor cultivated so fine a memory, nor have been able to do good to so many people."*

If you can swallow a toad every morning before breakfast, you are ready to do today's business.

—Old European Saying

SORROW AND SUFFERING

Happiness is good for the body but SORROW STRENGTHENS THE SPIRIT. There is a sweet joy that comes to us from sorrow. To love all mankind, from the greatest to the lowest, a cheerful state of being is required; but in order to have compassion and see into mankind, into life, and still more into ourselves, suffering is a requisite.

Think what we would miss without suffering:
Without pain, we should not know pity.
Without danger, we should not develop courage.
Without receiving injuries, no forgiveness.
Without affliction, no test for fortitude.
Without injustice, no occasion for forbearance.
Without violence, no training in self-control.

Adrian Anderson writes, "*For two decades the life of the great French artist Renoir was one of pain and misery. Rheumatism racked his body and distorted his fingers. Often when he held his brush between thumb and forefinger, and slowly and painfully applied his paints to the canvas, great beads of perspiration broke out upon his brow, because of his suffering. Renoir could not stand at his work, but had to be placed in a chair, which was moved up and down to give him access to the various parts of his canvas. Gazing at one of his favorite canvases, Renoir replied, 'The pain passes, but the beauty remains.'*"

A man's suffering and his happiness are evolved from within. Many of the greatest invalids have borne their suffering with cheerfulness and good spirits. Happiness is paradoxical because it may co-exist with trial, sorrow and poverty. It is a gladness of the heart, rising superior to all conditions.

Why do good men suffer? Without doubt, much suffering in the world is a result of violating the laws of man's nature which make for our highest good.

But suffering, in the case of good men, has entirely another mission. It perfects and ennobles character, enlarges capacity for sympathy and service, and fosters many of the most beautiful virtues and graces, such as mercy, sympathy, and human understanding. Good men suffer because WITHOUT SUFFERING THERE IS NO SUCH THING AS PERFECTED CHARACTER, and the releasing of compassion from the deeper realms of the soul.

It is the lot of man to suffer; it is also his fortune to forget and be happy. Nietzsche said, *"That which does not kill me, makes me stronger."* The size of human suffering is absolutely relative. It also follows that a very trifling thing can cause the greatest of joys.

Suffering is an alchemist, refining coarseness, transforming bad into good, changing pride into modesty, and selfishness into sympathy. This principle gives a sound foundation for a right theory of happiness. It also tells us why every hero, saint, and martyr, and the dear immortal few, were all made *"perfect through suffering."*

How much we owe to the gallant army of physically handicapped men and women who have marched in solid phalanx across the centuries bearing triumph on their faces and joy in their hearts. Every man must go through the fire. This means that during your lifetime you will experience great suffering or great sorrow, and you will need the help of God to win over your problems.

HOPE IS AN ELEMENT OF HAPPINESS

HOPE is a guide to good cheer and happiness. Hope keeps us with a song in our heart. The power of HOPE upon human exertion and happiness is wonderful. Hope is the ingredient that changes everything.

The three grand essentials to happiness in this life are SOMETHING TO DO, SOMETHING TO LOVE, and SOMETHING TO HOPE FOR. *"Hope itself is a species of happiness, and perhaps the chief happiness this world affords,"* wrote Samuel Johnson.

Happiness may be thrice-blessed: IN ANTICIPATION, IN FRUITION, and IN MEMORY. One pure and great source of happiness may be in looking forward; in HOPING to meet again those whom we have loved and lost.

My friend had been critically ill in the hospital. Several days after his operation I visited him. I found his face glowing with joy and he greeted me with a smile. *"My doctor has just spoken the five most inspiring words I've ever heard,"* he said. *"He came into my room this morning, put his hand on my shoulder and said, " 'You are going to live.' "* My friend told me that those five words worked magic in his life. It was as though he had just come out of a dark tunnel into bright sunlight.

You are in control of your life. Belief in the Supreme Power which is our source will give rise to HOPE, and HOPE is one of the most powerful stimulants to which the body can be subjected. A man can reach as high as his ideals. Jesus Christ is man's highest ideal.

Hope Is An Element of Happiness

"*Men often become what they believe themselves to be,*" admonished Mahatma Gandhi, "*If I believe I cannot do something, it makes me incapable of doing it. But when I believe I can, then I acquire the ability to do it even if I didn't have it at the beginning.*"

"*Everything that is done in the world is done by hope,*" said Martin Luther. The HOPEFUL MAN sees success where others see failure, sunshine where others see shadows and storms. The hopeful man believes that THE BEST IS YET TO BE, and paints in roseate colors the good times in prospect. Expecting and hoping are the whole of life. There is no medicine like hope, no incentive so great, and no tonic so powerful as expectation of something good tomorrow. GREAT HOPES MAKE GREAT MEN.

"*The men whom I have seen succeed best in life have always been cheerful and hopeful men,*" said Charles Kingsley, "*who went about their business with a smile on their faces, and took the changes and chances of this mortal life like men, facing rough and smooth alike as it came.*" Think WELL of yourself, as the world takes you at your own estimate. LIVE CONFIDENTLY.

"*It is worth a thousand pounds a year to have the habit of looking on the bright side of things,*" said Samuel Johnson. It is hope which maintains most of mankind. Press on, for victory's ahead. Be hopeful, friend, and win it. Everybody thinks of changing humanity but nobody thinks of changing himself.

"*Of all the forces that make for a better world, none is so indispensable, none so powerful as hope,*" says Charles Sawyer. The expression "We hope for the best," is an indication of faith in the future. In times of distress and uncertainty, HOPE has often lighted the way to better conditions.

FORMULA FOR HAPPINESS

Wise and great Goethe offers us "*Nine Requisites for Contented Living*":
1. HEALTH enough to make work a pleasure;
2. WEALTH enough to support your needs;
3. STRENGTH enough to battle with difficulties and overcome them;
4. GRACE enough to confess your sins and forsake them;
5. PATIENCE enough to toil until some good is accomplished;
6. CHARITY enough to see some good in your neighbor;
7. LOVE enough to make you to be useful and helpful to others;
8. FAITH enough to make real the things of God;
9. HOPE enough to remove all anxious fear of the future.

The happiest people have learned to be contented with what they have, never with what they are.

Abraham Lincoln had a simple formula for happiness: "*Don't worry; eat three square meals a day; be courteous to your creditors; keep your digestion good; exercise; go slow and easy. Most folks are about as happy as they make up their minds to be.*"

Jesus gave his FORMULA for personal happiness in the Beatitudes that apply to everyone. If by happiness we mean serenity, contentment, peace, joy, and soul satisfaction. HE TELLS HOW TO MEET EVERYDAY PROBLEMS WITH THE RESOURCES OF THE CHRISTIAN FAITH.

Laughter is the best medicine for a long and happy life. A good laugh does away with cares, worries, doubts, and relieves the great strain of modern life. Ethel Barrymore said, *"You grow up the day you have your first real laugh—at yourself."*

A pleasant disposition, a smile from within has a relaxing and healthy influence on the body. Let there be peace and harmony within at all times. *"Let not your heart be troubled,"* it reduces your living force. IT IS WORRY AND STRESS THAT CAUSES TROUBLESOME ACTION UPON THE HEART.

A French philosopher writes, *"The whole world is on a mad quest for security and happiness."* What everyone wants is the formula for continuous and genuine happiness. Like owning stock that doubles its value in a year . . . Having a healthy body and a healthy mind. Think happy thoughts, do happy things, associate with happy people. Have a good LAUGH EVERY DAY, even if it is over some ridiculous situation.

Always look on the bright side, cultivate cheerfulness, get all the funny stories you can and tell them to your friends. Learn to live a serene, happy, confident life, in spite of the jungle of frustration and confusion, for ceaseless stress and strain causes illness and unhappiness. *THE JOY OF LIFE IS IN LIVING IT.*

Poets and priests, philosophers and scientists, teachers, preachers and leaders of every age, have sought to work out a simple formula for "THE ETERNAL QUEST OF MANKIND—A HAPPY AND CONTENTED LIFE." For in the end, happiness is what all people want, regardless of the many ways they may seek it. *To be happy is the ultimate goal of all ambition, all endeavor, all hopes and plans.*

ENJOY THE BEAUTY OF NATURE

The art of happiness is to LEARN to APPRECIATE NATURE and LIFE. This gives the true meaning of life and happiness. Men live best upon a little; too many possessions run a man's life and he becomes a slave to the material things. The dominant force today is possessions. Nature has ordained all to be happy, if we would but learn how to use her gifts. *It's not how much we have, but what we enjoy, that makes happiness.*

All men have happiness as their objective, there is no exception. Were all men happy, violence would cease, for THE DAYS THAT MAKE US HAPPY MAKE US WISE. Happiness is a state of mind which is caused by the release of tension. Unhappiness is caused by the inadequate release of tension. Cheerfulness, good humor, and peace of mind are powerful elements of health. We are told that Lycurgus dedicated a little statue to the god of laughter in each of the Spartan eating halls.

Hawthorne believed, *"Happiness is a butterfly which, when pursued, is always beyond our grasp, but which, if you will sit down quietly, may alight upon you."*

Enjoyment is a state of HEART and MIND, by which we feel content and good with people and things. It is a stream of joy and peace that comes from the heart like a spring flowing out of the ground. This wholesome joy is spiritual and its serenity and pleasantness last indefinitely as it becomes a part of our nature.

From my earliest recollections I have had an affair of the heart with Nature. The voices of the night, the song of the brook, the wind in the trees, and the drifting clouds have always brought a message that has been understood and answered in my heart. My heart leaps up when I behold a rainbow in the sky. Stay close to the heart of nature and forget this troubled world.

A contributing factor to happiness is to be able to enjoy the gifts of nature. The poorest man living can enjoy these, for such blessings are free. Climb the mountains and get their good tidings. Nature's peace will flow into you as sunshine flows into trees. **ENJOY THE PRESENT!** If we cannot be happy with the present, how can we expect to be happy with the future?

"Though we travel the world over to find the beautiful," said Emerson, *"we must carry it with us or we find it not."* Sunsets and sunrises are so beautiful that they almost seem as if we are looking through the gates of heaven. One man will derive the keenest delight from scenery, trees and foliage, fruit and flowers, the blue sky, the fleecy clouds, the sparkling sea, the ripple on the lake, the gleam on the river, the shadow on the grass, the moon and the stars at night.

To another the beauty of nature is nothing. The moon and stars shine in vain; birds and insects, trees and flowers, river and lake and sea, sun, moon and stars, give him no pleasure.

"We do not sufficiently cultivate in children or—for that matter—in ourselves either, the sense of Beauty," said Lord Avebury, *"yet what pleasure is so pure, so costless, so accessible, indeed so ever present with us."*

THE RESULTS OF A HAPPY LIFE

RESULTS . . .
    Is this not what everything is all about?
    Is this not what your goals are for?
    Is this not what your life is all about?
    The result proves the right way to live.
    The result is the positive proof of the right
        solution and method.

Having a happy, loving attitude, a positive attitude, is mature health. This is the best state of psychological and spiritual health that can be obtained on this earth.

"*A merry heart doeth good like a medicine.*" Your family physician will tell you that JOY is a stimulating, purifying, life-giving flow which tends to keep all the secretions healthy, whose function it is to build healthy tissue from day to day. JOY LENDS ITSELF TO OUR BEST PHYSICAL AND MENTAL HEALTH.

Former President Dwight D. Eisenhower wrote, "*Unless each day can be looked back upon by an individual as one in which he has had some fun, some joy, some real satisfaction, that day is a loss.*" The hits of yesterday will never win today's ballgame. You have to keep on hitting. Just so in business, you have to keep on producing. What everyone wants is results.

Sometimes I think what we need more than anything else in our lives is SIMPLIFICATION. The most effective life is the life which is simplified, the life which is not crowded with complications. *So often our lives are so cluttered up with details and nonessentials that we haven't time to devote to the basic and important things like HAPPY LIVING.*

What has our materialistic life to offer man minutes after death? When Solomon said, *"Vanity of vanities, all is vanity,"* he meant that man tries to substitute material things which are shallow or futile for SPIRITUAL. Marie Ray wrote a beautiful thought that we should remind ourselves of each day: *"We have only the present moment, sparkling like a star in our hands—and melting like a snowflake."*

You will learn quickly that being busy is not everything. There is a VAST difference between being busy and being FRUITFUL. Some give the impression of working hard, but they are not accomplishing. RESULTS are what we are after, what our goal is.

If all I have said works, you will have another problem, which is to learn to measure your real wealth, not only in terms of money but in terms of HAPPINESS AND CULTURE AND GOODNESS.

Man discovers TRUTH through absurdity . . . through getting what he thought he wanted. In fulfilling his original dream he comes to realize all the things money can't buy . . . At the end, man comes to a realization that WHATEVER ONE IS, IS DETERMINED BY WHAT'S INSIDE, NOT OUTSIDE OF ONESELF.

THE ONLY REAL HAPPINESS AND POWER THAT IS MEANINGFUL IS THE POWER OVER ONESELF, AND NOT OVER OTHERS OR POSSESSIONS.

HAPPINESS IS NOT A REWARD . . . IT IS A CONSEQUENCE. HAPPINESS is not the end of life . . . CHARACTER IS!

CHARACTER INFLUENCES HAPPINESS

When life was nearly ended, as almost his final words, Horace Greeley said, *"Fame is a vapor, popularity an accident, riches take wings, those who cheer today will curse tomorrow, only one thing endures—character!"*

These words but remind us there is only one thing that really matters—building a life. He who achieves character can be neither feeble in life nor forgotten in death. Of a noble Greek, the people said, *"The goodness of the man is more than the Constitution"* When Paris was torn by revolution and bathed in blood, it is said of Lamartine, he never locked his door for his character was his protection. Even his enemies respected his goodness.

Emerson said, *"There was a certain power in Lincoln and Washington greater than their words."* Their noble character was what men feared and respected. Burke, that grand old man of English history, was mightier by far by virtue of what he was than what he said. Character—true, sterling, Christian character—is in itself success. Without it even the millionaire is a failure.

In the destiny of every moral being there is an object more worthy of God than happiness. It is character. And the grand aim of man's creation is the development of a grand character—and grand character is, by its very nature, the product of love and discipline.

Character is best formed in the stormy billows of the world. The grand aim of man's creation is the development of a beautiful character. Listen to the admonition of Lt. Gen. A. G. Trudeau: *"Character is something each one of us must build for himself, out of the laws of God and Nature, the example of others, and most of all, out of the trials and errors of daily living. Character is the total of thousands of small daily strivings to live up to the best that is in us."*

The qualities of character, hidden or buried, are revealed eventually even as the quality of a building is revealed under the stress of time and storm. When we do less than our best we cheat ourselves. We are the architects and builders of our own characters and must of necessity dwell within them. Character isn't built on ease, success, a million dollars or a happy life. Mainly through pain, sorrow and adversity are the bricks fashioned which can erect an enduring edifice.

There is a greater demand today for people of character than at any time in the history of America. As good character develops, happiness grows and flourishes. NOT EDUCATION, BUT CHARACTER, IS MAN'S GREATEST NEED AND MAN'S GREATEST SAFEGUARD. It is not what you learn, but what you BECOME. You can BECOME a kind, loving, joyful person of sterling character, Or you can become an EDUCATED DEVIL. That educational system is evil which produces bad fruit.

The earth holds many wonders, but the greatest wonder of them all is the man who makes it his first business to walk with God and fill his niche in the purpose of the Infinite. Well did Milton exclaim, *"A good man is the ripe fruit our earth holds up to God."* Character is everything to a man!

MOODS AND THEIR INFLUENCE

Your HEALTH is your most precious possession. Your efforts to learn the secrets of preserving health and avoiding sickness will be repaid with rich dividends. The teachings of science and the Bible reveal the interaction between moods and health and happiness.

Moods are an effect. In order to diagnose and cure, or to foster them as the case may be, we must locate their cause, also their nature. Some moods, like certain bugs in our system, are friendly and some are enemies.

The cause of vicious moods may be purely physical, or they may be mental, or they may be a combination of both. These two realms are very closely related.

That incisive psychologist, William James, assured us that the mind in all its moods superimposed itself upon the physical. By mind, Professor James means *"the seat and source of being,"* or exactly what the Bible means when it uses the word heart. *"Keep thy heart with all diligence . . . "* exhorts an Old Testament writer, then adds, *" . . . for out of it are the issues of life."* Also the passage which reads, *"For as he thinketh in his heart so is he,"* is announcing THE SAME LAW OF LIFE. The Apostle Paul's keenly put statement calls attention to the same law and shows its reaction on the physical: *"And the very God of peace sanctify you wholly . . . and soul and body be preserved blameless . . . "* And yet again, *"Whatsoever things are true, whatsoever things are honest, whatsoever things are just, whatsoever things are pure, whatsoever things are lovely, whatsoever things are of good report, if there be any virtue, and if there be any praise, think on these things,"* and *" . . . the peace of God, which passeth all understanding, shall keep your hearts and minds through Christ Jesus."*

These quotations from both science and the Bible are made for the purpose of showing one thing: *the heart, or mind, or seat of being, whichever word one prefers, directly INFLUENCES AND AFFECTS the whole man.* Have a happy, loving attitude. A positive attitude is mature health. This is the best state of physiological and spiritual health that can be obtained on this earth.

The word mood is defined as *"state or temper of mind resulting from passion or feeling."* Note the word "resulting." This definition is quoted for one purpose only: To keep before us the fact that a mood is the result of some state of feeling or passion which lies back of and gives rise to the mood, just as a spring gives rise to the stream that flows from it.

Disappointments are inevitable. Do not expect every plan you make to carry through without a hitch. Accept your disappointments. Smile even when things go wrong and speak pleasantly on all occasions. Experience has taught me that those who have no goals are candidates for the psychiatrist. They are empty inside, bored. A goal will stimulate excitement, enthusiasm, motivation, interest and effort. Few people realize how much of their happiness is dependent upon their goals.

"The soul and body," says a great medical authority, *"live so closely together that they catch each other's diseases."* In proof of his findings he says, *"Eighty percent of all physical diseases have their origin in or are enhanced by spiritual causes—such as worry, anxiety, fear and sorrow."* He goes on to say, *"Men are more sick in mind than they are in body."*

The causes of moods are listed by one physician as depleted nervous energy, worry, sorrow, illness, wrong blood count, liver out of order, poor elimination, malnutrition, etc. In fact, the list is almost endless. But the question is, are these things the cause or causes of moods, or are they the manifestations of a mood or moods? *Some people have hidden, self-destructive moods causing their unhappiness.* It may be we shall find the answer by looking at some of the things listed by the physician under the microscope of scrutiny.

Depleted nervous energy: That could come as a result of overwork. Is overwork a cause? Hardly. It is more likely to be a manifestation of inefficiency or pride or greed, stress or anxiety. "Keeping up with the Joneses" has sent more than one person flowers too soon.

The cure? Quit work this side of overwork. There is both sound sense and science in that exhortation given by the Apostle Paul, *"And having food and raiment, let us be therewith content."* CONTENT. That's it! *Content would prevent more physical crack-ups from overwork than any other remedy known.* And content is a quality of the heart. It is spiritual and therefore must take its rise from a spiritual fountain. *Most of us are more in need of a deeper sense of contentment with life as it is, than we are of a deeper understanding of life.*

Dr. William Hornaday admonishes, *"I am sure we are all aware of the power within us—the greatest moodlifter of them all, and that is to have a faith which is greater and be persistent. Work with it. Everything in life is earned. Love is earned, faith is earned, a position is earned. But we rejoice because we have the power to do it. And even a healing is earned. A healing of the body, a healing of the environment is* something that is earned, and we rejoice in the knowledge that it can be accomplished."

WORRY: Now here is a touchy point. But the diagnosis must go on. Worry is an obsession, a mania, an hallucinatory state usually superinduced by, dare I say, UNBELIEF. Several who are reading this have already died in a poorhouse at least twenty times! Strange, but true, most of the untoward things that have happened to the victim of worry have not happened to him. But he goes up to every turn in the road looking for calamity. If it is not there, well, he is sure it is somewhere, and goes right on looking for it. And that, in spite of the fact that experience has taught, or should have taught him, that *worry never righted a wrong, dried a tear or lifted a burden.* On the contrary, it has slain its tens of thousands.

WORRY IS UNBELIEF. And unbelief? Is there a cure for that? There is, and again, the cure is suggested by a scientifically accurate passage of Scripture: *"Therefore take no thought . . . for your heavenly Father knoweth that ye have need of all these things."* He feeds the sparrows, clothes the grass of the field, and tends the lilies. *"O ye of little faith . . ."* How much more will He take care of you! THE CURE FOR WORRY IS A HEART OF FAITH.

Lowell R. Ditzen writes, *"To achieve self-mastery we must face up to our fluctuating MOODS and try to prevent sharp changes of attitude. They can be caused by physical weariness or physiological deficiencies. They can be brought on by overexertion, too much pressure on our nervous and mental resources. When the clouds of depression start gathering, we must do something constructive to dispel them. The mind that can contemplate goodness will be prepared for such emergencies and provide some safety valve for the occasion."*

SORROW: Our long-drawn out sorrows are frequently self-pity carried to the point of complete absorption in self. Ego feeds on the cheap fodder of filched sympathy and grows leaner and leaner. Self-pity sits and mopes, never dreaming, it seems, that its whole attitude is self-defeating, insulting to God, and destructive to health. UNHAPPINESS IS AN ILLNESS, YOU MAKE YOURSELF UNHAPPY.

There is no need to carry this diagnosis further. The symptoms listed at the outset all point in the same direction: to a heart, either entirely or partially, out of tune with the Infinite. *All knowledge, as Plato pointed out, exists only that man shall discover his own divine nature.*

The conclusion of the whole matter is that the cause of the destructive moods is primarily mental and not physical. This determined, we are in a position to prescribe a remedy: a spiritual change at the seat and source of being. Such a spiritual change is accomplished, as the Apostle Paul would say, " . . . *be ye transformed by the renewing of your mind . . .* " and such a change will keep faith anchored in the deep water of abiding confidence.

Your rewards will be many: better health, greater physical and mental efficiency, and a happier state of mind. *The constant goal of every man should be to look for the good ways to live that are still possible. To seek out a healthier and a happier way of living, and the achievement of a better environment for his body as well as for his soul.*

In helping others, we shall help ourselves, for whatever mood we give out completes the circle and comes back to us. You can live a happier life by using a little common sense. Don't let yourself, or others, get you down.

Moods and Their Influence

There is no excuse for any intelligent person being at the mercy of his MOODS. A man must always keep himself in hand. Mental depression is a cumulative poison. Given an inch, it takes a mile. If allowed to take root, it grows like a cancer, tainting the whole mental life, and spreading its unhappy spell over everything. When we are criticized by others, it often throws us into depressed MOODS.

We should try to live in such a way that no one can condemn us justly. When just criticism comes, welcome it as something constructive. Like illness, unhappiness in all its aspects can be prevented! Nature has given equal opportunity of happiness to all, if we but knew how to use it.

Leading scientists and physicians all over the world are recognizing the tremendous part played by wholesome thoughts in the cure of many diseases and in the transformation of moral character . . . how conditions in the home can be changed, and how a man's attitude and relations in his business can be so altered that things run more smoothly and he himself be more successful. Thoughts have to do with the whole range of my life and your life. Our thoughts change our destiny. If happiness is to be ours we must learn to master our thoughts, for *"As a man thinks in his heart so is he."* We set the mood of each day by our attitudes and thoughts.

We must learn that it is natural for our friends and loved ones to be affected by MOODS, and to like or love them for what they really are, despite any unpleasantness of the moment. Unfortunately, when they are in a low mood, we often become exasperated with those who mean most to us in life, but we should know that moodiness is natural, and that we are all more or less subject to it.

CHEERFULNESS

In these days of uncertainties it is VITAL that we develop within us all the seeds of good and all that is best in us. *Get the habit of saying the cheerful, pleasant things.* Each day you need a good laugh, it is the best promoter of health, and is as friendly to the mind as to the body.

Cheerfulness gives a creative power which the pessimist never possesses. Use that strange power that comes with a cheerful, laughing spirit. *A cheerful disposition sweetens the day and smooths the road of life.* Always look for the GOOD in the other fellow; no one is perfect.

Count your blessings, be thankful and of good cheer. Being happy is a do-it-yourself job, no one else can be happy for us. THE GREATEST RESPONSIBILITY ENTRUSTED TO MAN IS THAT OF DEVELOPING HIMSELF. We must develop our inner qualities, for that is where our real wealth lies. Cheerfulness is a contentment that fills the soul, a state of joy.

Be active. Cheerfulness loves action, and philosophers agree that cheerfulness must include some form of worthy activity. Life demands work, but happiness requires dreaming, planning, aspiring, doing, and pressing on from one attainment to another still greater.

CHEERFULNESS is a great moral tonic. *As sunshine brings out the flowers and ripens the fruit, so does cheerfulness bring the feeling of freedom and life—develops in us all the seeds of good, all that is best in us.*

I WOULD GROW IN GRACE
AND STRENGTH
UNTIL I CAN ALWAYS...

1. SMILE in trouble, be a kind person.
2. LIVE so that my conscience will always approve my conduct.
3. GATHER greater strength in the midst of distress, let nothing disturb my peace of mind.
4. GROW brave by reflecting on the causes of past failure . . . meet my problems head-on.
5. LOOK into the future, figure out what's going to happen and how I can beneficially participate in it.
6. KEEP my heart firm in the few essential things which build Christian Character.
7. "DO UNTO OTHERS" as I would have them do unto me.
8. LISTEN! I can't learn if my mouth is making too much noise. Listening is a good habit, if you do a lot of thinking.
9. FORM the habit of expectancy. An expectant frame of mind attracts what we expect. EXPECT A MIRACLE!
10. WORK, because if honestly done, it is an investment in the eternal purpose of God.
11. THINK twice before speaking.
12. ACCEPT others as they are.
13. BELIEVE in and love the God who so loved me.
14. PURSUE principle, and do my best every day.

FAITH OR FRENZY

In a kind of frenzy too many of us rush through our days, not living life but consuming it. We are mere machines—victims of our high-pressure age. Our nervous excesses are responsible for more unhappiness than any other one cause.

The haste of modern living is waste in the truest, deepest sense. *We are so busy reaching for things beyond us that we miss eternal values which are near at hand.* In our hurry and fret we have forgotten how to walk and talk with God.

We have forgotten that solitude and growth are synonymous. THERE IS NO ROYAL ROAD TO DEVELOPMENT. Rush is the enemy of growth. Leaf by leaf the great oak grows into a sturdy tree. Forty years alone in the desert produced a Moses. Three years alone in the Arabian desert perfected Paul's vision. Christ spent thirty years getting ready for three years of ministry.

A healthy mind must be housed in an unhurried body. Professor Beecher used to tell the students at Yale: *"The first requisite is to take time."* Thomas Jefferson once said: *"Most men spend their time at nothing, other than hurrying about and never arriving anywhere."*

A doctor friend of mine stated, *"We do not deal with disease—we deal with errors in our life style. Straighten out your errors and you will be well."*

HAPPY IS THE MAN WHO HAS LEARNED HOW TO SUBSTITUTE FAITH FOR FRENZY, AND REST FOR RUSH.

BENEFICIAL INACTIVITY

To be unhurried, free from burning ambitions and little jealousies, is more than merely a wholesome state of mind, it is positively a blessed state of mind.

Most of us are more in need of a deeper sense of contentment with life as it is, than we are of a deeper understanding of life.

We have been so much with the business of living that we have forgotten how to live.

What most of us need is some time free from anxiety. . . .

Time to watch a pair of birds carrying flies and worms to a nest full of young.

Time to watch a squirrel frisk from branch to branch and from log to log with apparently nothing on his mind except to frisk.

Time to watch a hawk make lazy circles on widestretched wings as though practicing some graceful maneuver.

Time to sprawl on the grass or a bed of dry leaves in a patch of sunlight and watch the clouds sail away on mysterious voyages to far places across endless seas of blue sky.

Time to just think and dream of nothing until both heart and mind become so still that God can speak to us again of things that really matter.

"I went to the woods," Thoreau wrote, *"because I wished to live deliberately, to front only the essential facts of life and see if I could not learn what it had to teach, and not, when I came to die, discover that I had not lived."*

CHASING RAINBOWS

There's an old song I sang as a boy titled "I'm Always Chasing Rainbows." Today I believe more people are chasing rainbows. Very few people are CONTENT.

In our frantic chase for the rainbow, we toil for survival, raise families, and band together for protection. Everything in life has a price: success, education, love, friendship, material gain, fame, power, a relaxed mind, health—you name it. All things worth obtaining must be paid for. We save up for the day when we can sit and dream in the sun. And yet we are constantly driven by a restless urge for something more. We earn degrees to make more money. We try the untried in making love, in exotic drinks, in drugs and ego trips and gourmet foods. Still the urge persists for something more. Never enough! Never satisfied!

In our constant search for happiness and self fulfillment, the vast majority seek it on the lower mundane level of trying to find enough security, more sex, and sensual gratification, greater power, prestige and social status. *The real joy of life is to be found in daily striving toward worthwhile ends; in daily communion with loved ones; in frequent contact with friends, in daily deeds of service to God and man; in the battle with obstacles, and in daily victory over unworthy tendencies in ourselves.*

Real wealth is JOY and CONTENTMENT in the heart, plus the satisfaction of being useful by serving God and man. HERE IS THE POT OF GOLD!

TEN STEPS
TO BRIGHTEN YOUR LIFE

(1) Begin the day in a calm and cheerful mood: Say *"This is going to be a good day; I am going to be calm and cheerful right now."*

(2) Try smiling at others—make believe your underwear is tickling you. A smile is contagious and you will feel better as others smile at you.

(3) Count your blessings—list them one by one. Did you ever realize the real wealth you have?

(4) Enjoy this day with beautiful thoughts, pleasant memories. Live life one day at a time.

(5) Be adventurous. Try walking and seeing new neighborhoods, new buildings and parks, new scenery.

(6) Give a friend a phone call or write a letter. Tell him you are thinking about him; encourage him. Encouragement is oxygen to the soul.

(7) Be a happy person . . . see the bright side of life . . . shun gloom. Having a cheerful, loving attitude lends itself to your best health.

(8) Do a good deed; buy a book, or give something beneficial to a loved one.

(9) Give of yourself. Offer your services to a hospital, to a church; help people. The law of giving will reward you tenfold.

(10) Do the best you can each day; you are only living when you are useful and constructive.

TODAY

This is the beginning of a fresh new day, I greet it with HOPE.

Today comes only once, and never again returns, I must show my LOVE and be KIND.

God has given me this 24 hours to use as I will, I shall have a cheerful ATTITUDE.

Today is a great ADVENTURE, and well lived, makes every yesterday a memory of happiness and every tomorrow a vision of hope.

I must do something GOOD with this day, and not waste it.

This is my day of opportunity and duty, I expect something GOOD because I am going to help make it happen!

Today is a NEW DAY in my LIFE, a new piece of road to be traveled . . . I must ask God for directions.

Today I will be filled with courage and confidence, I must show my FAITH in God.

What I do today is very important because I am exchanging a day of MY LIFE for it.

The COST of a thing is the amount of MY LIFE I spend obtaining it.

When tomorrow comes, this day will be gone forever, leaving in its place something I have traded for it.

In order not to forget the price I paid for it, I shall do my best to make it USEFUL, PROFITABLE, JOYFUL.

APPRECIATION

Stinginess is not a matter of money alone. So . . .

Let's not be stingy with our appreciation when it is justly due.

Or with our words of praise where praise is due.

Or with encouragement when one has tried and failed.

Or with commendation when a job is well done.

Or with understanding and sympathy when another has been hurt.

Or with our service even where sacrifice is required.

Or with acts of love and kindness for toiling ones who become wearied with burdens along life's stormy way.

Everyone likes to be told that he is admired, respected, appreciated and liked. *"I like you because . . . "* and be ready to give definite, specific reasons.

The deepest principle in human nature is the craving to be appreciated. *If you have but a word of cheer, speak it while the one is alive to hear!*

"Withhold not good from them to whom it is due, when it is in the power of thine hand to do it." **Bible.** The best things of life are appreciated most after they have been lost.

Angels come to visit us, and we only know them when they are gone.

THINGS FOR WHICH I AM GLAD

I am glad for every sacrifice I have made that has given happiness to others and made their lives more livable.

I am glad that I have searched for TRUTH early and late. TRUTH is all I shall have when the sun sets on my years.

I am glad for all the hard stretches of road I have traveled. They have made me more appreciative of the easy places and of the beautiful vistas.

I am glad for the hard lessons learned under the rod of suffering. They help me now to cease my raving against time and fate, and rest in the sure confidence of a fixed faith.

I am glad for all the lessons I have learned out on the front lines of business, to do my best and not to chafe under misunderstanding. Truth always reveals itself if we wait.

I am glad that I have learned to laugh, even in the face of defeat. To inject laughter into tense situations is to save the day. For laughter calms tempers and soothes jangled nerves.

I am glad for the days I have had with nature in the deep, solemn forests; there I have heard and seen and felt God as is possible no other place on earth.

I am glad that I have been able, by the grace of God, to render some service so that a few may look upon me when day is done and say, *"he helped me."*

REAL WEALTH

Good health
A little common sense
A sense of God
A pleasant and confident attitude
A little love
A little good humor
A little cash

And you will be surprised how comfortable and contented you can be in a world where almost everyone is reaching for the moon.

It is not doing us much good to unravel the nature of the Universe unless we can unravel the nature of man.

We live in a day when so many are occupied with the "outer man," while the "inner man" perishes. The tendency today is to ignore man's inner nature and his eternal welfare, as if he did not have a spirit, a mind, or a soul. *"As the flower turns to the sun, so the soul turns to God."*—William Temple.

EVERY DAY
    YOU WRITE
        YOUR OWN
            PAYCHECK.

—*Alfred Armand Montapert,*
  DISTILLED WISDOM

RIGHT WORDS
BRING HAPPINESS

WORDS ARE THE MOST POWERFUL FORCE IN THE UNIVERSE. They are power releases for Good or Bad. Both Life and Death are in the power of the tongue. THOSE THAT SAY "I CAN" AND THOSE THAT SAY "I CAN'T" ARE BOTH RIGHT. Today many people have been taken captive by their own words. We can use our tongues to form the very words that defeat us, and even make ourselves ill, OR MAKE OURSELVES HAPPY!

To be happy you must bridle or control your tongue. The tongue is a mighty important little member of the body, but it can defile the whole body. It is unruly, evil, full of deadly poison. Your extremely negative words help to sink you, just like a hole in the ship will sink the ship. In Job 6:24 we quote, *"Teach me to hold my tongue. How forcible are right words."* TODAY, RIGHT NOW, YOU ARE THE SUM TOTAL OF WHAT YOU ARE SAYING WITH YOUR MOUTH.

God's Word that is conceived in your heart, then formed by the tongue, and spoken out of your own mouth, becomes a spiritual force, releasing the ability of God within you. In Mark 11:24 the Word of God says. *"What things soever ye desire when ye pray, believe that ye receive them, and ye shall have them."* Paul admonished, *"I can do all things through Christ which strengtheneth me."* THESE ARE POWERFUL WORDS.

We will talk about WORDS rather than thoughts as most words are spoken with little or no thought. Words are spoken out of a habit pattern, some are good and some are bad.

Many people who are defeated in life are defeated because they say the wrong words. They defeat themselves with the words of the enemy which are negative words. *"Thou art snared with the words of thy mouth."* We must be extremely careful with our words, for there is tremendous POWER IN WORDS. POWER FOR GOOD OR BAD.

Do you really want all the negative things you have been saying to come to pass? Are you conditioning yourself for good things or bad things? Everything you say may happen exactly as you say it. Choose your vocabulary carefully. Someone asked Albert Schweitzer what he thought was the greatest error of mankind. He replied, *"Men don't think."* Spoken words program you to either SUCCESS or DEFEAT.

Words are POWER RELEASES for good or bad. They CARRY FAITH or FEAR, and they produce after their kind. God's creative power is given to man in word form. YOUR CREATIVE POWER IS IN YOUR WORD. You can create a better life by speaking good and pleasant words. Everything God created He first spoke with words. *"Let there be light,"* etc.

WATCH WHAT YOU SAY! The things you say are the things that will manifest in your life. You have the God-given right to choose your own destiny. The mind rules the body and produces for us results, not according to facts, but according to our BELIEF. The mind is like the soil, it will grow what you plant, corn or nightshade (poison), good or bad.

God's creative power is given to man in WORD form. Your creative power is produced by the heart, formed by the tongue and released out of the mouth in word form.

Some people look for the worst in everything and find something to complain about in every situation in which they find themselves. A practical person will make the best of his circumstances. He will find something good in every situation in which he finds himself that he cannot improve. When talking to people always remember to be—KIND— COMPASSIONATE— THOUGHTFUL— UNDERSTANDING— LOVING— AND HAPPY.

Speak Victory in the face of apparent defeat. Speak abundance in the face of apparent lack. Whether you speak right or wrong, it is still a law.

This whole universe is pervaded and controlled with unseen forces called Natural Laws. If you want to read more about the Natural Laws, read my book on the 47 Laws of Life, titled, "The Supreme Philosophy of Man."

The Law of Cause and Effect, action and reaction, operates in the physical, mental, and spiritual realms. Therefore, your words should be carefully chosen as they can make or break you. These Natural Laws or unseen forces are the Laws of God and they are solid and unchangeable. *You don't break them, you break yourself on them.*

The spiritual law is based on the same basic principle of seed-time harvest. The words you speak are seeds that produce after their kind. If you plant potatoes you get potatoes, not corn. If you say negative words you will harvest negative results.

The tongue has the ability to destroy you or make you Happy and Successful in life. Out of the same mouth come blessings and cursing. WATCH YOUR WORDS!

It is much easier to be critical than it is to produce something better than that of which we are critical.

In the motion picture SOUTH PACIFIC there was a song titled *"Happy Talk."* People who are blest with happy talk actually live longer than people who don't laugh. Few people realize that health actually varies according to the amount of laughter.

The treasures of your heart cannot be hidden, but are manifest through your words. WORDS CONCEIVED IN THE HEART, FORMED BY THE TONGUE, AND SPOKEN OUT OF THE MOUTH ARE CREATIVE POWER.

How often a careless, unkind word spoken, can spoil your day, wreck some big job or deal, hurt a loved one, lose a friend. Many of us through ignorance, thoughtlessness, or want of judgment, hurt those we love best and wish to help. *If your heart has found happiness, don't let your tongue lose it for you.*

"May the words of my mouth and the meditation of my heart be acceptable in thy sight." (Psalms)

YOU!

The environment YOU fashion out of

... YOUR THOUGHTS ... YOUR BELIEFS

... YOUR IDEALS ... YOUR PHILOSOPHY

... IS THE ONLY CLIMATE YOU WILL EVER LIVE IN.

—Alfred Armand Montapert,
DISTILLED WISDOM

HAPPINESS IS A VACATION

We are greatly benefited in our general well-being, as well as in our work, by an occasional complete change of scenery and new places. Such is the adventure of taking a vacation. The benefits accruing from a vacation are many.

A vacation gives an opportunity for an overhauling of the physical mechanism. To get the best results from your vacation, plan a regular rest period during the day in which you completely relax. Let the world go by, hang loose.

To be avoided are parties, late hours, overeating, tiresome trips, mental worry. Bear in mind that recuperation depends primarily upon rest and relaxation, and especially in sleep. Relaxation, not exertion, should be your goal.

However delicious the food, do not overeat. Moderation is the golden rule of health. Eat plenty of fresh fruits and vegetables, drink copious amounts of water, exercise prudently, and strictly observe the rules of health.

Right mental attitude will do much to make your vacation enjoyable and beneficial. Cheerfulness, gratitude, and optimism are up-building influences. The good thoughts you radiate to others will come back to you in increased measure.

Ninety-nine percent of what we do, we do by HABIT. Getting away from the daily routine acts like getting a shot of adrenalin. It really makes us come alive. The prescription for health and well-being is to take a lot of short trips, in addition to the regular annual vacation.

When and where do you feel the happiest? Some of the happiest times of my life I have spent out in the woods where I was close to nature. We like the mountains in the spring and fall, where you hear the birds singing and breathe the fresh, clean air and watch the squirrels frisk under the majestic pine trees. In the summer months we love the seashore . . . we like to walk for miles along the beach in our bare feet. We visit the desert in the winter time.

Of most importance, a vacation is a break in routine—a change, a rest, a variety, time to relax, to unwind, to release tension. New ideas then come freely to mind. Vacations are skipped by some people because they entail a break in routine. But that is exactly the most important reason for taking them. To keep things inside us from going stale we need a fresh look now and then. An occasional break in routine is essential to progress. Away from the office or the factory, and away from day-to-day routines, our thoughts flow into new channels. A time for contemplation, for stock taking. Are we satisfied with our accomplishments? Our plans? Our ambitions? It's a time for fresh thinking.

It is by seeing, comparing, judging, valuing, analyzing, selecting, that men keep abreast of the opportunities of the times. If the change entailed in a vacation throws one out of gear for a time, it must be remembered that this is the best thing that can happen to anyone. His regular routine no longer a part of him, one can view things objectively, with the balance and impartiality of the objective point of view. Worries and troubles do not loom so big now. Possible pitfalls are noticed, and opportunities for improvement and betterment previously unseen come into view. It is a larger and better world that one comes back to from a vacation.

The readjustment of the point of view and the highly productive thinking done on one's vacation are not the least of the benefits accruing from a vacation. A wise doctor once advised an important executive that his worst defect was lack of leisure moments in which to view, calmly, his problems. *If a man is to do the best work of which he is capable, he must stop work occasionally and think.* The man who works continuously at a white heat pace does not obtain nearly the results of the one who stops at times to deliberate. Today man's life is hurry up and hurrah, a rapid transit dash through a complex maze of obligations, demands, promises, schedules, mental notes and budgets.

A bit weary of it all? Lost the vision? Well, be daring enough to take the trail that leads to solitudes. Pitch your tent in some deep, shadowy valley where it is almost dark by day, and where the stars show yellow above the firs at night. Wait until out of the shadows comes the strange calm which will give you eyes to see and ears to hear. For the first time in years, it may be you will discover that God is in His world, and—like His world—He draws near to those who draw near to Him.

Travel provides a change in climate and scenery, which is often more necessary for certain ailments than medicine. Although travel may be considered the richest of all pleasures, it may also be considered a good investment. For a successful vacation take along less clothes and more money.

PLAN TO MAKE YOUR VACATION THE BEST YOU EVER HAD. Health improvement is the major consideration. Have a written outline for what you will do to build a reserve of robust health so that you will return to your regular occupation with inspiration, full of pep, mentally and physically refreshed. *Good health is a priceless possession and must be earned and maintained.*

AN ACTIVE MIND CAN KEEP YOU YOUNG

You will stay young longer by keeping your mind active. Man has three divine dimensions: physical, mental, and spiritual. Each one of these must be constantly looked after, whether you are in your twenties or seventies.

"USE IT OR LOSE IT" is nature's dictum.

You can be just as productive mentally at eighty as you were at twenty, provided you keep your mind active, and you have not had any disease that affects your mentality. Be extremely careful in your daily mental habits. You would not be so foolish as to eat poisonous food deliberately instead of pure food. Then why try to nourish your mind on an inferior mental diet?

If you do not exercise physically, you get muscle laxity; the same applies to your mental ability. Stretch your mind and you will keep in good mental condition. Keep your mind alert, young, happy! Happiness is wholeness of personality. Nurture your mind with good wholesome thoughts, read worthwhile books, and you will find that intelligence actually increases as one grows older. Remember the mind controls the body, and a strong, determined attitude can alter physical illness.

THE CONSTANT PURSUIT OF SUCCESS AND FAME can eat up your whole life. You also come to believe that you are more important than you really are. Very few people die a natural death. They kill themselves by their way of life. Moderation appears to be a lost art.

HAPPINESS REDUCES STRESS

Life is full of irritations. Our tensions mount, and first thing we know we are loaded with STRESS that has the power to destroy our enjoyment of life. STRESS IS THE RESPONSE OF THE BODY TO ANY DEMANDS MADE UPON IT.

STRESS IS DANGEROUS. It triggers certain glands to function in the body that create hypertension and build cholesterol, and too much of that is not natural. So you start the deterioration of your body. The relationship of the stress mechanism to cardio-vascular disease is well documented.

To live a long time and to enjoy life, the unseen force we must develop is the PROPER ATTITUDE. Develop the ability to deal with life in a RELAXED rather than a TENSE manner.

Drastic and dramatic changes are taking place NOW . . . socially, politically, industrially, personally and economically. These changes will be very confusing and stressful. Today man is continually walking a tight rope trying to cope with these changes. What he desperately needs, when caught in these swift currents of change, is a SOLID ANCHOR or a FOUNDATION on which to build and hold.

Science has proven that stress is a killer. We live in an age of anxiety. And because we are confronted with more and more situations that produce stress, increasing numbers of Americans at younger ages are suffering from high blood pressure, heart attacks and strokes. Furthermore, all of us must deal with our own emotional upset and tension caused by the everyday pressures of living. Is there anything we can do for ourselves to relieve these tensions and prevent such illness from occurring?

Yes, the simple meditative and prayer technique can help everyone. *The development of our spiritual dimension is the world's greatest need today! It can bring you inner peace and calm.* It is easily learned and has no side effects. What more could we want from a natural method of beneficial treatment?

Your Creator designed you for a purpose. Be natural, the ULTIMATE IN LIFE IS TO BE YOURSELF and to develop your spiritual nature. Dwight L. Moody admonishes: *"The world has yet to see what God can do WITH and FOR and THROUGH and IN a man who is fully consecrated to HIM."* It's a challenge every day to DO your best, BE your best, and you shall HAVE the best. *DIFFICULTIES, PROBLEMS, CHALLENGES are the names given to the things which it is our business to overcome.* Our body has a certain amount of vital life force depending upon the care we give it. You can spend it foolishly or preserve it wisely and live longer. If anything BUGS you, get rid of it. Don't worry about things you can't do anything about.

Stress will disappear like icicles melting in a hot June sun if you RELAX, be natural, develop your spiritual dimension, for there is where you get your real peace of mind. Put your trust in God, the Higher Power. Every intelligent person believes in the Higher Power.

The regular practice of meditation is another way to lower blood pressure. Anything that lowers blood pressure without undue side effects is beneficial. Lowered blood pressure leads to a lower risk of developing atherosclerosis and its related diseases, such as heart attacks and strokes.

Tensions are at a minimum when we are happy. We must stand up to these tensions and stresses to develop our mental and spiritual muscles. You are in control of your life. Belief in the Supreme Power which is our source, will give rise to HOPE, and hope is one of the most powerful stimulants to which the body can be subjected.

Don't take yourself so seriously, be more light hearted and less serious, learn to laugh at yourself in almost any situation and you will become a better person.

Dr. Hans Selye, world expert on "stress," says, "*A motor car doesn't suddenly cease running because of old age. It stops because of failure of some part that has worn out. It is the same with people. Under continuous stress—either physical or mental—some vital body part gives way, leading to a variety of illnesses, and eventually to death.*" When asked what are the worst stresses, Dr. Selye would say, "*Anxiety, worry, frustration—especially hatred and jealousy. Most people are their own worst enemies—unconsciously bent on self-destruction.*"

NATURAL LAWS

Every Person Has Free Choice . . .

Free to Obey or Disobey

THE NATURAL LAWS.

YOUR CHOICE Determines the Consequences.

—*Alfred Armand Montapert,*
THE SUPREME PHILOSOPHY OF MAN

GOD'S HAPPY WORLD

THE WORLD I LOVE IS . . .

> The world that God molded into mountains and plains.
> The world through which He cut deep canyons for rivers and in which He linked up the mountains in chains.
> The world in which He turns to palette and brushes and carefully paints each scene.
> . . . Hills that are done in purples with tracings of yellow and green.
> . . . Meadows and valleys and pastures that glow with immortal sheen.
> . . . My Palace built by God's own hand, pillared and roofed with green, bedecked with blossoms rare and fresh.

I HATE THE WORLD THAT MEN HAVE MADE . . .

> With its toil and moil and greed.
> With its smoke and grime and smells.
> With its rush and sweat and pretense.
> With garbage trucks in the streets and tin cans on the curbs.
> With its war, intrigue, and duplicity.
> With its murder of men for a price and lyingly calling it patriotism.

I HATE man's world.

BUT I LOVE WHAT GOD CREATED!

TRUE EDUCATION BRINGS JOY

THE TRUE PURPOSE OF EDUCATION IS THE HARMONIOUS DEVELOPMENT OF ALL OUR FACULTIES; AND THE FIRST OBJECT OF ANY LEARNING IS THAT IT SHOULD SERVE US IN THE FUTURE. We can become wise in many ways, yet all too often our learning does not directly contribute to the improvement of character or peace of mind, or gain us a basic understanding of values.

If we believe these statements, why don't we acknowledge and develop the spiritual kingdom as part of our educational process? We recognize three kingdoms now: MINERAL, VEGETABLE, and ANIMAL. A fourth one should be added: the SPIRITUAL KINGDOM. WHEN WE DO THIS WE SHALL HAVE EDUCATION AT ITS BEST.

The mistake is—and ever has been—to think of the physical man as the real man, and the physical world as the real world. The real man, the Scripture insists, is the spiritual man, and the real world is the spiritual world. The mind is the door to the heart. It is with the heart that we believe. Man has a soul. The soul is the total you of you, the seat of being. The Bible calls it heart. We make our decisions in our heart.

The great danger in public education today is that we have failed to see the difference between knowledge and wisdom. We train the head and let the heart run hogwild. We allow culture and character to walk miles apart, stuffing the head with mathematics and languages—leaving manners and morals out of the picture.

True education is the harmonious development of all our faculties. Reading, writing, arithmetic, and grammar do not constitute education any more than a knife, a fork, and a spoon constitute a dinner. It seems that we can develop a kind of philosophy which enables us to gain some distinction or knowledge, *but does not enable us to cope with the daily issues of living. Many well informed persons are in a constant state of inner agitation and fail to enjoy inner peace and happiness.* The most important thing has not been learned—HOW TO CONDUCT OURSELVES SO THAT WE MAY TRULY LIVE.

Religious education, including the basis for morality and the ways in which we distinguish between right and wrong, is the basic foundation of all useful education. Our relationship to God is the most important thing we can learn. The great central fact in human life is the coming into a conscious, vital realization of our oneness with Infinite Power, and the opening of ourselves to this divine inflow.

The important thing for us is not so much a comprehension of the totality of God as it is to discover the necessity for our own spiritual development. *Spiritual life is the emancipation of what we are. Through a spiritual life we become responsive to God. On that level, we become responsive to God. On that level, and on that level only, do we find release for our highest powers and qualities.* THE REAL FUNCTION OF EDUCATION IS FOR COMPLETE LIVING.

Billy Graham writes, "*You can put a public school and a university in the middle of every block of every city in America—but you will never keep America from rotting morally by mere intellectual education. Education cannot be properly called education which neglects the most important parts of man's nature. Partial education is far worse than none at all, if we educate the mind but not the soul.*"

Jesus taught that life must be centered in God; that our happiness is dependent upon our holiness; that our union with God is our hope of fulfilling the ultimate purpose of life. This way of life teaches us to think God's thoughts, speak His language, and how to live the life we were created to live. BY SO DOING, WE SAFEGUARD OURSELVES AND THE SOCIETY OF WHICH WE ARE A PART.

Modern society has committed the fundamental error of disobeying the law of spiritual development. Our greatest need now is to develop the soul. Never were we more in need of being made whole. With this development we are free to enjoy to the highest degree the beauty, order, and permanence of the universe. We are free to dedicate ourselves in service to others. We are free to commune with nature and find in that communion the ties to the universe that we have always sought.

THIS IS TRUE EDUCATION AT ITS BEST!

David Sarnoff writes, *"Education worthy of its name is not merely an intellectual process. It is no less a spiritual process. Its purpose is not only to pile up knowledge and skills, but to ennoble man's soul. Rarely in the past has there been such an urgent need for the kind of insight and understanding that we call spiritual."*

As individuals we cannot change the world to any great degree, but we can build a world of our own within ourselves, and it can be Happy and beautiful. I hope to see the day when investigators in the realm of biology will be as honest with their facts and as honorable with the truth as they are with reference to these other kingdoms or realms. They never have been. That's one reason why the present generation is such a mess. *Because we have deliberately withheld from all these youths nearly all our scientific evidence and truth of the spiritual realm, and a spiritual life that is as real as any other realm.* Until we are true to those facts, we cannot be said to actually, literally, and truly teach biology.

What sculpture is to a block of marble, education is to the human soul. Education means experience and faith, courage and understanding—and, most of all, the ability to think and act. Herein lies the importance of education. I say education rather than instruction, because it is far more important to cultivate the mind than to store the memory. Studies are a means and not an end. The development of general ability for independent thinking and judgment should always be placed foremost.

We teach our children that they descended from lower forms of animals, and that they are nothing but a sophisticated animal with a brain; that our impulses and emotions stem from jungle situations and are not authentic human experiences. *We neglect to teach them the truth that man is a spiritual being born of God in His image. That our true potential for life accomplishment, for meaning in life, is in the development of our spiritual dimension.* Until we see life from this viewpoint, there is nothing worth living for except creature comforts.

God gave each man a bundle of gifts. Your work should be according to the gifts He has given you. Ask yourself, "What did I do with the gifts God gave me?" Gift of serving, gift of giving, gift of leadership, gift of happiness, etc.

Most of our present day personal and national problems stem from our spiritual inadequacies. The key to any problem is to get at its root cause. The lack of spiritual development is the root cause of our present unhappiness. Someday we will have the opportunity to repudiate this whole anti-God set-up in this nation. Then it will be possible for God to do for this nation and us individually what He cannot do under present circumstances.

Some day science will get around to admitting that God is the measure of the Universe, and that man at his best is an elemental and potential measure and a revelation of God. Then, for the first time in several thousand years, we shall have education worthy of the name. Alfred North Whitehead in his *"AIMS OF EDUCATION,"* says, *"Any educational program that omits emphasizing religious and moral principles is incomplete."*

True education is the total development of the total man—body, mind, spirit. The wholesome development of his ambitions, aspirations and emotions. The mature application of these qualities to his work, his play, his home life, his community life. To be mature, adjusted, contributing vital personalities, should be the goal of all true education. The question to be asked at the end of any educational step is not what has the person learned, BUT what has the person BECOME? To become the WHOLE PERSON you are capable of becoming is the ULTIMATE IN LIFE.

All learning should lead to the fact that it is the individual educating his inner life, to the degree that it can govern his outer life, and properly handle everything that comes his way. Believe me, dear reader, THE END OF ALL KNOWING IS NOT WISDOM, but PERFECT FAITH. ESSENTIAL KNOWLEDGE is therefore but PERFECT FAITH. FAITH in a living God, living in your heart, is LIFE and LIFE ETERNAL. TRUE EDUCATION MEANS TREATING THE WHOLE MAN: BODY-MIND-SPIRIT.

THE HAPPY CHOICE

Nothing ranks a man so quickly as his skill in selecting things that are really worthwhile. Every day brings the necessity of keen discrimination. Not always is it a choice BETWEEN GOOD and BAD, but often it is BETWEEN GOOD and THE BEST. In the nobility of our thoughts, and the purity of our actions we determine the quality and the extent of our future. Character is choice in blossom and achievement is the ripe fruit. By an unalterable law men are paid back in their own coin—with interest. Noble thoughts and wise choices are reactionary.

The things which we allow to control our lives mold us into their own image. Our choice of good or evil is the choice of life or death both here and hereafter. NOBODY EVER DID, OR EVER WILL, ESCAPE THE CONSEQUENCES OF HIS CHOICES. Right relation to God forms the basis of both reward and punishment.

Wendell Phillips, when a student at Harvard, heard the voice of three million slaves crying for freedom. The cry forced a choice. The choice was elective. It was between a career, wealth and fame, and a selfless service for a defenseless minority. He chose the latter. His choice wrote his name in God's Hall of Fame.

Beaumont was a man of rare genius. He lived almost beside Shakespeare. Of him Dr. Samuel Johnson says, *"His mind was keen and brilliant. He could have had a place with immortals."* But he chose secondary things. He lived and died with trifles. Shakespeare was less brilliant but he hitched his wagon to a star. He lives; Beaumont passed with his death. *The distinction is not so much a distinction of intellect but the ability to choose between first class things that abide, and second class things that perish.* This POWER TO CHOOSE is what makes each one of us an individual—a god in his own right. And our CHOICES determine what happens to us; what our future will be—happy or unhappy.

All the promises of blessings and all the warnings of punishment are based on the scientific principle that the harvest is determined by the seed sown. What shall the harvest be? We have only to look at the seed which we are sowing. *There is no magic by which even God can save anyone from the consequences of his wrong doing.* The sooner we see and practice this truth, the sooner we shall have an intelligent conception of Christianity.

An intelligent person can no more escape the conclusion that sin is suicide and unholiness is hell, both in nature and degree, than he can escape the fact of his own being. We speak of God punishing sin. That is basically untrue. *Sin is its own punishment just as righteousness is its own reward.* Men and nations sink or soar, survive or perish as they choose to be dominated by sin or righteousness.

Most of us can, as we choose, make of this world either a palace or a prison. Successful living depends upon the choices you make. You have to know what's important and what's unimportant for you. Intelligent choice implies a realistic sense of values.

Men can know more than their ancestors did if they start with the knowledge of what their ancestors had already learned. This is why a society can be progressive ONLY if it conserves its traditions.

Our prime motive in all things is the attainment of satisfaction and joy. The whole universe is pervaded with unseen forces called Natural Laws or Laws of God. Man's whole being is pervaded with unseen forces called the Laws of Man's Nature. These Laws are invisible but are as real as the physical Law of Gravity. Motives are also invisible but are the true test of character. My friend, God's world is geared to righteousness. But He made you a free agent, GAVE YOU THE POWER OF CHOICE. You have the choice of living a mediocre life or the abundant life.

Life is actually made up of our choices. We are the sum total of them, and if we hold to an attitude of love and thanksgiving for all the good things within our grasp we may have what all ambitious people long for—SUCCESS AND HAPPINESS.

IT'S ALL UP TO YOU HOW YOU USE OR ABUSE IT.

"God is the greatest democrat the world knows, for He leaves us free to make our own choice between evil and good."—Mahatma Gandhi

---

SUCCESSFUL MEN

Successful men usually snatch success
    from seeming defeat.

If they know there is such a word as failure,
    they will not admit it.

They may be whipped but they are not aware of it . . .
    THEY FIGHT ON.

    That is WHY they SUCCEED!

—Alfred Armand Montapert,
THE SUPREME PHILOSOPHY OF MAN

THE NATURAL LAWS OF LIFE

The whole universe, including Man, is controlled by unseen forces called Natural Laws. The whole universe is geared to righteousness. All of the natural laws lend themselves to this.

The universe is orderly. What if the sun had free choice like man, and would rise at midnight or sleep till noon, or go on strike? Nature, which has no choice, is dependable, responsible. The whole universe operates on Law and Order, the days, the seasons, the sun, moon, stars, gravity, electricity, chemistry, physics, etc.

But man, who has the power of free choice, has disobeyed the Natural Laws and has messed things up badly. Crime, terror, deterioration, disaster, and insecurity are the result. Free choice, and the Natural Laws, provide the consequences to man's acts. The Law of Cause and Effect operates in the moral, mental and spiritual realms, just as surely as it does on the physical plane where we see and understand it.

The only way man will ever get out of this mess is to return to and obey the Natural Laws, which are the basic cure, the answer. BUT the cry today is *"Do your own thing!"* Every act of our obedience to God's laws lends itself to the achievement of happiness, contentment and joy. HAPPINESS IS THE CONSEQUENCE. Violate the principles and laws of the universe and you will get in trouble.

It is man disobeying the Natural Laws and the myriad man-made laws that is causing man to have one foot on the other man's neck. Today we have an infinite network of man-made laws managed by a vast hierarchy of attorneys and politicians. MAN HAS MOVED FURTHER AWAY FROM NATURE AND NATURAL LAWS.

From time immemorial God's problem has been to get man to look from HIS VIEWPOINT, obey His unseen forces or Natural Laws. Man's failure in this particular problem is the reason for the condition of the world today. "The Natural Laws of Life" are the KEY to man's highest and best living. The KEY to education and life at its BEST! They will reveal to a person that he is living in a world of natural law and order. That these unseen forces which pervade the universe are real and that man never breaks these Laws, he breaks himself when he disobeys or violates them.

Man today will protest that he has risen from primitive man to the highly civilized, cultured man that he is now. But we ask, what have we accomplished for the good of man's life, for the good of his soul? Have we eased his mind? Have we produced harmony and serenity within?

It is natural for man to overlook the obvious. Goethe said: *"The last law man will learn will be the laws of his own nature."* In our so-called enlightened generation, very few people even know the laws of their own nature. Yet most of our problems stem from the nature of man.

TRUE LIVING IS LIFE UNDER LAW . . . man flowing through the universe upon the currents of Divine Law, like a ship moving on the great currents of the ocean. The wise man does not desire to escape from Law, but aspires to perfect harmony with it. *"Fishes,"* said Confucius, *"are born in water, man is born in the Law. If fishes find ponds they thrive; if a man lives obediently in the Law he will live his life in peace."*

FRIENDSHIP BRINGS HAPPINESS

A FRIEND IS A PERSON . . .

. . . With whom you can be sincere.
. . . To whom you do not need to explain yourself.
. . . To whom you never need to defend yourself.
. . . On whom you can depend whether present or absent.
. . . With whom you never need pretend.
. . . To whom you can reveal yourself without fear of betrayal.
. . . Who does not feel he owns you because you are his friend.
. . . Who will not selfishly use you because he has your confidence.

I WOULD HAVE SUCH A FRIEND . . .
AND I WOULD BE SUCH A FRIEND.

Much happiness and peace of mind in our lives depends upon making a wise choice of our friends and companions.

OPPORTUNITY

THE PASSING HOURS, DAYS AND YEARS

BRING OPPORTUNITIES WHICH QUICKLY PASS

GRASP THEM NOW—OR LOSE THEM!

—*Alfred Armand Montapert,*
DISTILLED WISDOM

FRIENDSHIP

Some of the most lonely roads I have ever traveled have been the most crowded roads. And some of the most pleasant roads I have ever traveled I have traveled alone. Or, with one person whose friendship was so real that it did not need bolstering even with words.

Come to think of it, that is what makes some roads so lonely—too many words and too much noise. And apropos of all of this, there are few things more dangerous to friendship and peace of mind than too many words. Indeed, few friendships will survive endless words and continuous noise.

Silence sometimes makes itself felt sooner and deeper than words. You can declare your love until the declaration ceases to ring true. What you FEEL, you make others feel. The most satisfactory road then is the road where silence broods and where thoughts are the language that hearts feel and understand. How little we know some of our friends, or even some of our relatives. Members of the same family often live in practical isolation; their minds move as if they were in parallel lines and never meet; they are not really ever in touch with one another.

One can have many acquaintances but few friends. We should be discriminating in our choice of friends. . . . for man becomes, and in surprisingly short order, like the company he associates with.

"I shall pass through this world but once. Anything, therefore, that I can do, or any kindness that I can show to any human being, let me do it now. Let me not defer it nor neglect it, for I shall not pass this way again," admonishes Etienne de Grallet.

WHAT DO YOU WANT FROM LIFE?

Just what do you want personally from life? This is one of the most important questions you will ever consider. Try the plan of writing out in definite statements the things you really desire to BE and to DO and to HAVE.

What will you achieve with your life: business or professional success? A substantial income? Friends? Influence in your community? Standing in your chosen field? FAME? POWER? POSITION? SECURITY? LOVE? SPIRITUAL SATISFACTIONS? What?

You can have just about whatever you want—if you want it badly enough, and are willing to sacrifice for it. The world will give you nothing without extracting its price. By your nature, as well as the laws of the universe, you cannot receive or be given something for nothing. That is not the scheme of things. Take what you need. But pay for it you must, in one way or another.

The plain truth is this: First, you have to MAKE UP YOUR MIND what you really want. Second, are you willing to pay the price of attainment in study, work, sweat, effort, and money?

If the price of attainment is too great for you to pay, your desire is not strong enough for you to have it. DESIRE is the POWER behind your effort. Little effort—little results; big effort—big results. It's as simple as that.

The question becomes: are you willing to pay any price that is required? Is the thing you seek of supreme value? THE

COST OF ANYTHING IS THE AMOUNT OF YOUR LIFE YOU SPEND IN OBTAINING IT.

Your desire sets the limit of your attainment. The price you are willing to pay is the measure of what you will get. This applies to anything—you name it. Money, power, possessions, even answered prayer. You can achieve and have only that which you develop within yourself.

Learn the A-B-C's: *Awareness-Before-Choice.* If you wish consciously and consistently to make wise happy/pain decisions, you must use the formula: AWARENESS BEFORE CHOICE. Your power of self-control develops self-esteem and more JOY in your life. The wisest choice is to develop your ability to think rationally.

You were born a unique individual. Then why copy others? Why follow the herd? *Be yourself, use your God-given talents and you will be happy and successful. If you are offering what everyone else is offering, who needs you?* Get from where you are now to where you want to be: with friends, loved ones, finances, and all other areas of your personal world. Your chief goal is spending your life experiencing HAPPINESS and JOY. If you do this, your life will be useful and constructive and profitable. We should always look forward, and NOT look back—unless we can benefit from lessons in the past.

Man is inherently designed with certain powers, faculties and perceptions. Each man is responsible for the proper use, or misuse, of these powers, talents and abilities. It is a person's responsibility and duty to himself, to his world, and to the external Power in which he exists, to govern his tempers, subdue his appetites, refine his emotions, inform his mind, and increase his understanding.

There is a price tag on everything. The greater the happiness you wish to achieve, the greater the price you must pay to achieve it. This is derived from the Natural Law of Cause and Effect—Action and Reaction. A weak man believes in Luck, but the strong man believes in Cause and Effect.

Analyze at the start, the price of anything you desire. Is it necessary, is it worth its price? The price may be in many different forms or combinations, such as time, energy, money, discomfort, illness, health, or even eventual death. Is it worth the price? That is the big question.

Everyone has the desire to make his life better and happier. The question we ask ourselves is, what can I do to reach this goal? What can I do to acquire knowledge and develop wisdom, to cope with change and the disarray of life, to get along with people, to learn how to solve problems, to serve my family and my country, to become a better person, to grow old happily?

Men and women have gone by many ways to seek a happy life. Some have failed because they set themselves no definite goal, but drifted here and there, always hoping to come upon a land of their vague dreams. The secret of a successful and happy life is to plan and do, plan and do.

In our world of pretense it is necessary to keep a low profile. Don't flaunt what you have. When you keep a low profile you will help prevent people from becoming envious of you. Most people are envious or jealous if you have something they don't have, or if you are successful. Success is envy's hell. After you acquire your low profile you will have a better understanding of what this phrase means, *"The meek shall inherit the earth."*

Shakespeare has one of his characters admonish, *"The fault, dear Brutus, is not in our stars but in ourselves, that we are underlings."* We are short on FAITH not to believe that there is immeasurably greater knowledge and power in God, and also within ourselves.

If the heart of you is in fellowship with God you will be fifty percent happier, fifty percent more prosperous. It is a paying business to walk in fellowship with God. You have thought of prayer maybe as something indulged in by weak-minded folk. *When you intelligently pray you are using one of the great scientific forces in this world which makes for a clear intellect for you, and a wholesome, healthy body, and a normal, wholesome walk on the level that you were created to walk.*

The man who prays intelligently will be more courageous, more contented, more industrious, more productive. If your prayer does not lift you to that realm, then your prayer is simply a mockery. If prayer is real, it will do every bit of that for you. No wonder Roger W. Babson, the greatest business statistician, said, *"The greatest undeveloped natural resource is the souls of men."* He was right. If prayer makes men more healthy, more courageous, more industrious, it does exactly what it is supposed to do.

We do not need prayer to influence God on our behalf, we need prayer to RAISE US UP TO THE LEVEL where all God's blessings flow in abundance. On this level, prayer becomes the ATTITUDE indicated by Jesus Christ when He said, *"Only BELIEVE, and thou shalt see the glory of God."* When the heart and mind of man are in harmony with the Creative Spirit that undergirds the universe, man has new resources for EFFECTIVE LIVING!

I HEARD
A HAPPY BIRD NOTE

Funny, isn't it, how trifling a thing will stir a memory that belongs to a distant past and superinduces a mood. I heard a bird note. Just a snatch of song that wafted through an open window as the songster winged past my study. But something in that fragment of song awakened a memory and transported me to a far place—almost two thousand miles from where I am sitting at my desk.

A place guarded by treacherous green marshes, standing thick with rushes, out of which runs a languid creek, turned the color of rust by the soil along its banks.

A marsh above which I have watched emerald, gold and amethyst dragonflies sparkle like magnets of light, and listened to the haunting notes of the hermit thrush when evening sips golden wine from the chalice of an amber sunset.

A marsh which becomes vocal with frog music when night has thrown her sable garment over the shoulders of the hills, and the whippoorwills join the chorus with their staccato-like notes which serve to emphasize the legato of the deep-voiced frogs. *From my earliest recollections I have had an affair of the heart with nature.*

A marsh which would be considered forbidding by some, but which afforded me many a day of solitude, and where I drank deeply of the tonic of strength offered by nature to those who worship at her far altars.

I Heard A Happy Bird Note

A mellow breeze fragrant with the kiss of first spring flowers stole through the open window and caressed my face. With eyes closed, I tilted back in my chair and listened to the "little voices" that whispered of far-off places. In unspeakable content, bathed in the warm fragrant flow of mellow air and with the memories pouring in upon me, I dreamed and felt supremely happy and luxuriously satisfied.

The bird winged on its way. His song lingered. Fifty years it carried me back. Carried me back until, like waters warring with confining banks, my heart—rebellious and aloof—is left warring with present restraints and limitations.

But I've had an hour of communion with yesterday, and it has enriched my today . . . thanks to a seeming trifle. Such trifles, like so many little things, take on size as they affect and influence the heart.

A song will outlive all lectures in memory. It is delightful to transport oneself into the spirit of the past, the memories that give meaning and depth to our lives. *Milton, grown old and blind, drew from memory the finest thing he ever wrote. Longfellow reflected that the years agone furnished him the material from which he created the finest poems. Muretus says that it was the story of Seneca's incredible memory that inspired him to his greatest achievements.*

You can trace your life with songs. I remember where I was working, and the condition of the times, when many songs came out. I used to sing them, whistle them. The song *"Memories"* has very beautiful words. The song *"Remember"* . . . I can recall the man singing it at the Hippodrome Theatre, the only day I ever played hooky from school, about 1917. The past is the bank in which we store our most valuable possessions . . . the memories that give meaning and depth to our lives.

A HAPPY PRESENT

There is perhaps, in all literature, no picture of a satisfying, replete, or happy present so graphically and poetically sketched as the word picture given by David in the Twenty-Third Psalm.

The mountains in the distance lean, light-washed and cloud-crowned, against an early morning sky. Fingers of light, two hours ago, lifted the curtain of night from a sleeping world, and the morning star melted into the dawn. A thousand dewdrops, cradled on leaf and grassblade, caught the first rays of the sun and wreathed their transparent faces in flashing smiles.

The birds, in one great burst of song, made martial music for the marching feet of day, and the brook that flowed through the pasture set rippling fingers to the keyboard of its mighty organ and played open diapason, while columns of light came rank on rank. Hillside and valley flamed with blossoms of a dozen hues, and the willows along the stream shook out their green hair in the first breath of breeze.

A flock of sheep has spread itself over the pasture like the rolling tide of a mighty ocean of silver, and the clouds have spread their sails for the voyage of the day. Lambs stray from their mothers and come galloping from their explorations, like tiny puffballs of white and black blown in by the wind. Their scampering feet flush a thousand grasshoppers that rise in a variegated rush on wings of green and yellow, brown and gray gauze. Contented bleats roll in a soft chorus from wooly throats, while the shepherd reclines dreamily against a sun-warmed stump, listening to a song sparrow's merry lay as it sits atop a cherry bush, and to the poignant call of the meadowlark that has chosen for his rostrum the topmost rock of a huge stonepile.

The sun climbs higher and higher, and heat, like a spreading blanket, covers pasture and flock. One after another the sheep drop in the high sweet clover and dreamily chew the cud.

And there, my friend, you have a pen-picture of God's replete present. A satisfying replete present is necessary for two very important reasons: First, the heart of each one of us can know contentment in no other way. Second, we can be permanently useful in no other way. Our heart union with God liberates us from the pangs of heart hunger, and brings us to the banqueting hall of a plentiful present. The "heart" of living a full, rich, satisfying life depends upon our oneness with God.

The only IDEAL you'll find in this world is the ideal you carry in your heart. When we lose our ideal then we are ready for burial. Life knows no tragedy like the loss of an ideal. Disillusionment, certainly. Disappointment, surely. Failure in part, yes. But life knows no tragedy like the loss of an ideal. Without an ideal the soul dies. In a word, the secret of a man is the secret of his aspiration. Solomon had so well said, *"Where no vision is the people perish."* And they perish because there is no lodestone to pull them up to what they were made for and to inspire them with things beyond them.

THE HAPPY MAGIC TRAIL

Across the creek from our little cottage, a trail wound over the hill and disappeared among the trees. Like all trails that cut their way through the forest this one intrigued me. The lure became irresistible, and so one day, in answer to the beckoning call of late afternoon shadows, I made my way across the pasture to where this trail steals mysteriously through a screen of vines and begins to ascend the hill.

It was a new trail. I did not know what to look for. Each turn and hill and valley was, therefore, a thrilling adventure. Each tangled vine, each tree, each bed of wild flowers, and each bunch of feathery ferns was a discovery.

Life is like that. Each day is a new road. Like the Prophet of old, the morning warns us that we *"have not passed this way before."* **IT IS THE LURE OF THE UNKNOWN THAT MAKES LIFE A THRILLING ADVENTURE.**

If our days were all mapped, and scheduled, life would soon become an unbearable monotony. It is the arrangement of a wise Providence that the road may reveal itself only as it is traveled. There is something of the pioneer in all of us, and the cultivation of this pioneer spirit is essential to progress whether it be in religion, education, statesmanship or what not. Blessed is the person who will not allow himself to become an echo or a faint carbon copy of a bold original, for verily I say unto you he shall be saved from a "yes man" attitude of mind, which is absolutely destructive of personality and initiative.

To know something of the road ahead might, at times, be an advantage, but these advantages would be offset by the fact that knowledge of what awaits us around the next turn would, many times, make dull and uninteresting what otherwise might be a thrilling discovery.

Not only so, but knowledge of what lies ahead would frequently so terrify us that we would have no courage to go on. If fortune tellers and seers could reveal the future I would not visit them. I would prefer to allow each bend in the road to reveal its own joy or sorrow.

Sometimes many days must come and go before one can get far enough away from human sounds to become one with the supreme and unemotional forces of the forest. Once the confused echoes of a swarming blind humanity are lost amid the solemn quiet of the far places, one experiences a homecoming unlike anything else earth has to offer. Hills and valleys, crags and bracken, trees and clouds take on a tenderness deeper than lies within human power to give and there is a hospitality surpassing the best efforts of even the perfect host.

Woodland trails have a lure all their own. Not only do they rest, charm and rejuvenate the person who learns to answer their call, but they will show one, better than any other teacher, how nature works her enchantments.

THE HEART HAS A WAY of meeting each emergency as it presents itself, WHETHER IT BE JOY OR SORROW, success or seeming failure, and, as Tennyson would say, the heart . . . fills us with *"the glory of going on."* Experience with the years (no matter, at this moment, how many; one may live much in a few years, or little in many years) has made me more and more certain that this philosophy of life is much more satisfactory than any scheme calculated to reveal the future could possibly be.

Visions of a great tomorrow thronged my mind with promise of world-startling achievement, but for the most part these visions move on ahead. And this is well. If it were not for these dreams of future achievement, middle life would have long since become a drab monotony.

Disappointment has met me at more than one bend in the road, but out of the darkness a new sunrise of courage has given strength against another day of battle. And so the years have brought me quickly on to middle life through changing scenes and strange vicissitudes.

Looking back I can see the road winding through sunlight and shadows; over hills, and down into the valleys; along an easy, level place, and then up a steep and difficult climb. But these vicissitudes have all had their advantages; they have increased my checking account in the bank of experience, and I am drawing on this account for the duties, responsibilities, and opportunities of a present which would be bankrupt in courage were it not for the sunny, shadowy, sorrowful, joyful yesterday.

I turn toward the west. The road is hidden. Yonder I can see the dim outline of the last hill silhouetted against the shadows of the evening sky. With trembling hand—not from fear, but from the excitement of breathless, expectant wonder—I shall one day part the curtains and pass from sight into the great unknown. What does it hold? I do not know; only that the Master, with whom I have journeyed, is there, and with Him, the unnumbered years can but mean adventurous living. Toward the last bend in the trail then, I hurry on, buoyed up by the hope that yet more thrilling experiences with life await me.

A HAPPY LIFE

We are not in this world merely to get rich, or gain fame or power, or to become learned in the arts and sciences, or to build a great business.

All of these, or any of these, may be among our duties, and they may fill our hands. But in all our occupations the real business of life is to put our complete trust in God, and to grow LOVING in DISPOSITION and NOBLE IN CHARACTER.

We may learn the finest arts of life: music, painting, sculpture, poetry; or may master the noblest science; or by means of reading, study, travel and conversation with refined people, attain the best culture. But if in all these we do not develop our spiritual dimension and attain a oneness with God, we have missed the greatest prize of living. The secret of happy days is not in our outward circumstances, but in our own heart life.

Be happy . . . give thanks . . . happiness plus gratitude equals JOY. My advice to people is that they find joy in their daily lives. Some always look for gloom and despair . . . even when they have no real problems. The joy of living depends upon you.

If in the midst of all our duties, cares, trials, joys, sorrows, we are not day by day growing in faith, love, gentleness, unselfishness, thoughtfulness, compassion, and in all the higher branches of life, then we are not learning the great lesson set forth for us by our Master in this school of life. *Life isn't worth living—YOU have to MAKE IT WORTH LIVING.*

CONTENTMENT

Most of us are more in NEED of a deeper sense of CONTENTMENT with life as it is, than we are of a deeper understanding of life. THE SECRET OF CONTENTMENT IS KNOWING HOW TO ENJOY WHAT YOU HAVE.

The art of contented living is like all arts, it must be learned and practiced with incessant care. Many people get the insistent feeling that their life is unproductive; restlessness and discontent fills their mind.

In this day and age, GREED is the dominant force. Apparently we can have too many desires. Listen to what some of the wise men have to say on contentment:

Thomas Fuller admonished, *"Contentment consisteth not in adding more fuel but in taking away some fire; not in multiplying of wealth, but in SUBTRACTING MEN'S DESIRES."*

Joseph Addison wrote: *"A contented mind is the greatest blessing a man can enjoy in this world."*

John Balguy wrote: *"Contentment is a pearl of great price, and whoever procures it AT THE EXPENSE OF TEN THOUSAND DESIRES makes a wise and a happy purchase."*

Sir James Mackintosh remarked, *"It is right to be contented with what we have, but never with what we are."*

Rochefocauld writes, *"When we cannot find contentment in ourselves it is useless to seek it elsewhere."*

Lin Yutang wrote, *"The secret of contentment is knowing how to ENJOY WHAT YOU HAVE, and be able to LOSE ALL DESIRE FOR THINGS BEYOND YOUR REACH."*

A Chinese proverb states it this way: *"A MAN whose heart is NOT content is like a snake which tries to swallow an elephant."*

Confucius says: *"With only plain rice to eat, with only water to drink, and with only an arm for a pillow, I am still content."*

Socrates summed it all up when he said: *"CONTENTMENT is natural wealth."*

"My cup runneth over." (Psalms)

Contentment comes to the man who lives with an unfaltering faith in an unfailing God. The person who lives with eternity in his heart will find a strange calm and strength in his spirit.

One of my brothers finds happiness and contentment in buying things. My wife is happy when she is reading books, her Bible, and making those with whom she comes in contact happy. My mother too was most happy when the family was all together. There were ten of us and we are a very happy family. I find happiness in my life style, as I am enjoying the luxury of leisure, good health and peace of mind.

Joy and contentment are indeed precious qualities which very few experience in their lives. Reaching for the moon represents a characteristic of our society. The person who knows how to enjoy life will never grow old no matter how many years he can call his own. It is easy to be happy at specific times, but THERE IS A CERTAIN ART IN BEING HAPPY AND CONTENTED EVERY DAY.

THE HAPPINESS OF SPRING

Yeah, it has me—Spring Fever . . . I want to walk along a trail that meanders among the trees to cool itself off.

I want to listen again to the voice of silence.

I want to worship where words and music and preaching are not necessary.

I want to forget . . . Out where nature makes me remember essential things.

I want to feel the wind in my face, the dew on my hair, and the presence of God like a warm air in the shadowy places.

I want to converse with things that have no spoken language and hear words that are not defined in the dictionary.

I want to be alone with more company than one can have in a crowd.

I want to empty my mind by filling it so full of nothing that there will be no room for thoughts.

I want to be awakened by a wash of light that does not remind me of a day all scheduled, arranged, and chartered.

I want to watch the landscape of springtime. Its beauty thrills my soul. While some may scheme and others toil, I love to sit and gaze.

I want to lie on my stomach and drink water from a brook that has not been made "safe" to drink by those who are so much concerned with my health that they finally kill me.

I want to pick and eat berries, watercress and wild cherries that have not been sprayed with bug poison until they taste like brown paper soaked in kerosene.

In short: I want to get away from the mess that men have made, and live in God's world for awhile.

****

I AM HAPPY AND GRATEFUL FOR MANY THINGS, BUT MOST OF ALL FOR DAYS AND NIGHTS I'VE SPENT . . .

With just a trail to follow and the campfire's friendly glow, out where the rock-ribbed mountains are white with eternal snow.

With trees when the evening breezes were whispering a lingering goodnight to trembling boughs.

With the stars when they shine through the dark like candlelight flickering behind thin curtains.

With the birds settling to roost among the thick branches of a cedar and softly chattering like children afraid in the dark.

With the sound of running water that fills the night with music that no artist can set down in notes.

With the flickering light of a campfire making shadow pictures among the trees when the first stars come out to play hide-and-go-seek with clouds that reflect the silver of a rising moon.

With God who speaks most loudly in the voice of silence, and who reveals Himself most clearly when veiled in the darkness of a forest night.

SEEKING HAPPINESS

While crossing the Atlantic one summer on the Queen Elizabeth II, I had the opportunity to carefully read my Bible and mark up my favorite scriptures.

In reading through Ecclesiastes I read where Solomon, the rich, wise ruler, tried everything under the sun to see what would satisfy him and make him happy. Solomon was considered the wisest man of his day. Perhaps we too can learn a vital lesson if we will listen to this great and wise man. Solomon gives his practical experience in successful living. Our objective is to increase our happiness and learn to live a rich full life. We may even decrease the amount of our suffering.

NO MAN SOUGHT HAPPINESS WITH MORE INGENUITY AND PERSISTENCE THAN SOLOMON. He tried all of these avenues and found them wanting. In his book, Ecclesiastes, we read:

"I made me great works; I builded me houses; I planted me vineyards; I made me gardens and parks and I planted trees in them of all kinds of fruit; I made me pools of water to water therefrom the forests where trees were reared; I bought men-servants and maid-servants, and had servants born in my house; also I had great possessions of herds and flocks, above all that were before me in Jerusalem; I gathered me also silver and gold, and the treasure of kings and of the provinces.

"I gat me men-singers and women-singers and the delights of the sons of men, musical instruments, and that of all

sorts. *So I was great, and increased more than all that were before me in Jerusalem . . . and whatsoever mine eyes desired I kept not from them; I withheld not my heart from any joy . . . then I looked on all the works that my hands had wrought, and on the labor that I had labored to do; and behold, all was vanity and a striving after wind, and there was no profit under the sun."*

At the end he said, *"Vanity of vanity, all is vanity."* Meaning ALL these things are temporal, passing, futile.

After Solomon explored many realms for happiness, he says, *"Here is my final conclusion . . . Fear God, and keep His commandments, is the whole duty of man."*

Ultimate happiness is found only on the spiritual level. While the physical realm has its joy and satisfaction, the highest level of happiness comes only from the spiritual realm. The reason is very simple: each of us is more a spirit being than a physical body. We were made in God's image in that each of us is a living soul, destined to exist eternally. This being true, only when we are rightly related to God can we be really, constantly happy.

G. K. Chesterton summed it all up: *"Joy is the gigantic secret of the Christian."* Make it a Way of Life for you. Joy makes you feel good inside.

Most people have the idea that happiness is something that can be manufactured. They do not realize that it can no more be manufactured than wheat or corn can be manufactured. It must grow; and the harvest will be like the seed. "Like produces like" is a Natural Law—God has never put an apple on an orange tree.

GROWTH

Because a thing helped you once is no sure sign it will help you again. Growth means PROGRESS and DEVELOPMENT. Progress and development mean CHANGE. Baby food will not sustain the full vigor of manhood. Change of diet calls for ADJUSTMENT. Ability to make necessary adjustment is a—perhaps I should say the—mark of healthy, normal growth. You might check by this rule and determine whether you are treading up and down on one spot or whether you are going some place.

And, too, remember that *growth is always a painful process.* You have to be jostled, kicked, pushed and frequently blasted out of old ruts. Whoever can rouse you to new ways, thoughts, methods and studies is your greatest benefactor.

Charles R. Gow wrote, "*What is life all about? Development . . . growth. The two great laws of life are growth and decay. When things stop growing they begin to die. This is true of men, business or nations.*"

Too, the person with whom you most violently disagree is the person who may do you the greatest good. He makes you THINK and thinking is the thing many of us need most—but do the least.

We frequently mistake endless talk for deep thought. To merely discuss a matter is no proof that you have thought on it. It frequently is proof that you have NOT thought. *True living means THINKING, OBSERVING and LEARNING.* It recognizes the difference between TRUTH and TRASH, that THE QUALITY OF LIFE IS MORE IMPORTANT THAN LIFE ITSELF.

CREDO

I BELIEVE IN AND LOVE . . .

NATURE, in all its moods and aspects, and a more profound respect for man as he seeks to labor together with God for the highest good of humanity:

The silent places where the forest whispers
    and a running stream reflects the shadow . . .
Stately trees that stand silent and worship-
    ful, like a congregation engaged in prayer . . .
The living friendship of flowers and shrubs
    and the comradeship of grass and ferns . . .
Clouds that sail through turquoise skies,
    like dream-ships putting out to sea . . .
Little paths that wander here and there,
    as though in search of a trysting place . . .
The rustle of autumn leaves,
    and the sound of a falling nut . . .
The early frosts and dry, stark limbs, be-
    cause they speak to me of spring and resur-
    rection . . .
The first experimental note of a bird when
    dawn washes up out of the East like a huge
    gray wave . . .
Goldenrod holding torches of yellow to light
    the way for the retreating feet of summer . . .

I BELIEVE IN AND LOVE all these things, because they come to me from the Giver of "every good and perfect gift." And most of all, I believe in and love God who so loves me.

THINK HAPPY NOBLE THOUGHTS

What one thinks determines what he will SAY and DO. A person cannot afford to think bad or negative thoughts. We become what we dwell upon. Present thoughts determine my future. This is a natural law that is just as real as the law of gravity.

Paul knew the human mind and character very well. He said, "*Whatsoever things are true, whatsoever things are honest, whatsoever things are just, whatsoever things are pure, whatsoever things are lovely, whatsoever things are of good report; if there be any virtue, and if there be any praise think on these things.*" (Phil. 4:8)

F. G. Burroughs gives his expression of Paul's thought:

Think noble thoughts if you would noble be;
Pure thoughts will make a heart of purity;
Kind thoughts will make you good,
    and glad thoughts gay,
For like your thoughts, your life will be alway.

Whate'er is true and reverend and just,
Think o'er these things,
    and be like them you must;
Of good report, of lovely things and pure,
Think, and your mind such nectar shall secure.

    Think much of God and you shall like Him be,
        In words of faith and hope and charity;
        Protect His image from all foul abuse,
        and keep the temple holy for His use.

We can eliminate a lot of unhappiness in our life if we know how to control our thoughts. We have the gift of choice, of free will. We can choose our thoughts! Let us cultivate the habit of joy. *A merry heart is better than medicine.*

We can never see the sunrise by looking into the West, nor can we live the beautiful life we are supposed to live—if we think negative thoughts. The classic remark made by wise Solomon is a profound truth. *"For as a man thinketh in his heart, so is he." (Prov. 23:7)*

Wilfred A. Peterson writes, *"Almost all the trouble in the world is created by things people think, say, and write. Words of anger, malice, hatred, resentment, jealousy, like physical blows, cause people to hit back. Overbearing, demanding words create determined resistance. And the attitudes of mind back of them, even though we do not speak the words, are sensed by others. For the telepathic power of thought is no longer merely a theory. Thoughts are things."*

Never at any time get yourself into a negative state of mind, or allow a friend to lead you to a point of agreeing to anything that is negative. Do not pick up "hot bricks." The minute you enter into negative thoughts, they have pulled you down. This is a practical law, proven over and over again. Never lose that positive attitude, the positive mind you have. A POSITIVE APPROACH TO LIFE IS A CARDINAL POINT FOR HAPPY—SUCCESSFUL—DYNAMIC LIVING. MAN'S GREATNESS LIES IN HIS POWER OF THOUGHT.

That the mind has great power over the body there is not the slightest doubt. To consciously think that "I CAN" impels the subconscious faculties into action. Life is formed from the inside out. What I am inside determines the issues in the battle of life.

LOVE IS SUPREME HAPPINESS

TO LOVE AND BE LOVED IS THE GREATEST HAPPINESS OF EXISTENCE.

The law of love is one of the natural laws of life, the greatest and deepest law of all. It fills the hearts of all those who seek it with kindness and compassion. It is the central theme in the laws of life, for love is cement that makes men whole.

By love we mean love of life, love of God, love of people, work, beauty, learning, nature, animals. There are two types of love. "Agape" is the love that builds up. "Eros" is the selfish love that tears down. One is constructive, the other is destructive.

How does one practice love? By kindness, respect, unselfishness, attention, patience, understanding, and trust. Each of us is born with the capacity for love, which takes many forms. It can be love for family, home, friends, country, possessions, power, fame, Divine love. The visible signs of love are without end: Love is a puppy snuggled inside of a little girl's raincoat; a blanket being tucked around a sleeping child; the Hallelujah chorus, a beam of light through a stained glass window, a lump in the throat when the flag goes by. Love is the light and sunshine of life.

Alexis Carrel said, *"The greatest single force in the world is love."* Love will smooth out all your wrinkles. It will put a new spirit into your body, bring a new light into your eyes.

Vincent van Gogh wrote, *"There is the same difference in a person before and after he is in love as there is in an unlighted lamp and one that is burning. The lamp was there and it was a good lamp, but now it is shedding light, too, and that is its real function."* In this life we have three lasting qualities—faith, hope, and LOVE. But the greatest of them is LOVE.

We are so constituted that we cannot fully enjoy ourselves, or anything else, unless someone we love enjoys it with us. Even if we are alone, we store up our enjoyment in hope of sharing it thereafter with those we love. Love lasts through life, and adapts itself to every age and circumstance: in childhood for father and mother, in manhood for wife, in age for children, and throughout life for brothers and sisters, relatives and friends. LOVE GOES WITHOUT THAT ANOTHER MAY HAVE.

"Though I speak with the tongues of men and of angels," says the Apostle Paul, *"and have not LOVE, I am become as sounding brass or a tinkling cymbal. And though I have the gift of prophecy, and understand all mysteries, and all knowledge; and though I have all faith, so that I could remove mountains, and have not LOVE, I am nothing."* Love and Life are the two most wonderful things in the world. Enjoy both to your full capacity.

Victor Hugo wrote: *"The supreme happiness of life is the conviction that we are loved."* Love is to life what sunshine is to plants and flowers. Love is more precious than gold.

FAITH—HOPE—LOVE

and the greatest of these

is LOVE. *(I Corinthians 13:5)*

SILENCE FOSTERS HAPPINESS

There is no explanation quite so effective as silence. Explanations rarely explain. Those who demand explanations usually have their opinions formulated before you begin to explain. IF YOU ARE RIGHT YOUR LIFE WILL DO ITS OWN EXPLAINING. IF YOU ARE WRONG YOU CAN'T EXPLAIN. So, go calmly on your way and forget everything but the business of right living—and let time explain you.

The older I grow the more I see the value of silence. Sometimes you conquer by yielding, and say the most by keeping silent. There may be a time to speak—but it is so difficult to know when to speak and what to say.

Shakespeare admonished, *"Men of few words are the best men."* We are bombarded by words all day long. Words affect our emotions, which in turn affect our body chemistry. If you have something good going for you, KEEP QUIET!

Pythagoras admonished, *"Be silent or let thy words be worth more than silence."* The wisest retort is often silence. The words of a silent man are never brought to court.

Benjamin Franklin said, *"I gave silence second place among the virtues I determined to cultivate. Considering that in conversation knowledge was obtained rather by the use of the ears than of the tongue."*

The harvest is not ripened by the thunderous forces of nature, but by the secret, silent, invisible forces. So the best qualities of our spiritual lives are matured by quietness, silence and the commonplace.

General De Gaulle advised: *"Nothing more enhances authority than silence. It is the crowning virtue of the strong, the refuge of the weak, the modesty of the proud, the pride of the humble, the prudence of the wise, and the sense of fools. To speak is to dilute one's thoughts, to give vent to one's ardor; in short, to dissipate one's strength; whereas, what action demands is concentration. Silence is necessary preliminary to the ordering of one's thoughts."*

The difficulty is that those who do most of the talking have nothing to say, and all too frequently those who do have something to say, say it at the wrong time. No wonder Solomon observed: *"Words fitly spoken are like apples of gold in pictures of silver."*

"I have often regretted my speech, but never my silence." (Cyrus) Happy also is the man who makes a daily practice of silence in his heart that he may hear God speaking.

QUALIFICATIONS FOR SUCCESS & HAPPINESS

FIRST is a big waste basket.
        You must know what to DISCARD.

SECOND, it is as important to know what to PRESERVE.

THIRD, do not offer, nor accept, un-
        necessary RESPONSIBILITIES.

FOURTH, learn HOW and WHEN to say NO.
        For developing the power
        to say NO gives us the
        capacity to say YES.

DIFFERENCES IN PEOPLE

People are individual entities, each has unique qualities. Today people and organizations, schools, etc., are trying to "shape" everyone into one mold. This situation causes much unhappiness. This way people lose their individual traits and innate characteristics.

THE IDEAL SITUATION IS TO HAVE EACH INDIVIDUAL EXPRESS HIS GOD-GIVEN TALENTS BUT KEEP IN HARMONY WITH HIS ASSOCIATES. This applies not only to individuals but families, organizations, and even nations. Everyone has something to contribute. Differences are certainly divisive, but can they not also provide a richer, more cohesive whole, because of themselves? I DON'T BELIEVE IN UNIFORMITY!

You get the maximum benefit by using the essential differences between people which help contribute to a much richer result or goal. One person may be good at ideas, innovation; another at diplomacy; another at practicality; another at friendliness, warmth; another at seeing the result of the whole picture, the future; another who can decide whether the bridge should even be built, and if so, where and when. All expressions add up to a more satisfactory, diversified whole. People's interests don't always run parallel, BUT THEY MUST KEEP IN HARMONY even though they do not think the same way.

Differences make for a more satisfying, diversified whole. Even countries and nations are different in cultures, in opinions, in skills and abilities, and national characteristics. The British are noted for innovation, the French diplomacy, Dutch pragmatism, Italians warmth, Germans discipline.

The Government and the schools all try to equalize people, to fit them into a mould, to make them carbon copies, parrots, echoes, but this is wrong. People are different and have different talents, skills and abilities. The organization that's going to get to the top is the one that has the best people who work in harmony, in concert like a great symphony orchestra. *Talented people working together in harmony is the unbeatable combination for the success of any individual enterprise, or nation.*

Our modern society is sick with the disease of conformity. People are afraid of being different. The rewards for being different are easily recognized. As a basic factor the general demand is for individuals whose performance is above average, and therefore different. No one is any better than you, but you are no better than anyone else until you do something to prove it.

Herbert Hoover wrote, *"Honest differences of views and honest debates are not disunity. They are the vital process of policy making among free men."* There are a thousand million different human wills, opinions, ambitions, tastes, and loves; that each person has a different history, constitution, culture, character, from all the rest.

HARMONY is the keyword—COMPROMISE is a way of life. One never finds Utopia or complete agreement. We must learn to LIVE IN HARMONY with the DIFFERENCES that unite us. If we want to keep HAPPY we should refrain from making harsh judgment of a person. SO LET US ALL WORK TOGETHER AND BE HAPPY!

BALANCE IN LIVING

Look for all the good ways to live that are still possible. You can give fifty women the same ingredients to make a cake and the cakes will all taste different. What makes the difference? It is all in the mix.

The difference in the quality of life between people is the mix. And by mix, in human sense, I mean a person's attributes, thoughts, attitudes, heredity, beliefs, values, ideals, Philosophy, quality, and balance. People are a mixture of temperaments, a variety of traits of character.

BALANCE, says the dictionary, *is equal poise of the two sides of a scale*. The two important words in the definition are EQUAL and POISE. A scale is easily thrown out of balance.

As with scales, so with character. It, too, is easily thrown out of balance. Some can tell you exactly how almost anything ought to be done, but they never do anything—out of balance!

Philosophers, from the ancient Greeks to Buddha and Balzac and Pascal and Pitkin, have been extolling a balanced life as the most happy life, and many unhappy people can—when they face the issue—trace their discontent to imbalance.

Some forget that honesty is more than a matter of "paying your debts." If they owe you money they will repay you, but it never occurs to them that debt of gratitude or appreciation is just as binding—out of balance!

Some seem convinced that the reason why they cannot get along with others is that they are so gravely misunderstood by everyone. The real reason is they themselves are OUT OF BALANCE.

Some forget that when they change environment they must take themselves along with them. Their trouble really is not with environment—it is with their own *lopsided character—OUT OF BALANCE.*

Some think so long from one viewpoint that they finally convince themselves that there is no other viewpoint and consequently get out of balance. LET'S GO IN FOR ADJUSTMENTS—what say? To leave the scales out of balance too long will finally ruin them.

We are always wanting to do more. Balance is what is needed, not too much or not too little. One-half of the things people do is brought on by our own egotistical desires. MODERATION IS ONE OF THE MOST IMPORTANT WORDS IN THE DICTIONARY.

It is our responsibility to keep in GOOD HEALTH, live a long time and not wear ourselves out by always trying to catch the carrot or the brass ring. Stick to what you know best! "*Shoemaker, stick to your last,*" is a great truth. Good advice. COMMON SENSE IS THE MOST IMPORTANT ELEMENT IN LIVING.

A lot of rich men die poor. Because of greed they lose their money, which they earned mostly the hard way. *Many times one's enthusiasm will chloroform his judgment!* We know when we meet a well-balanced woman or man. Such a person conveys to us a balancing influence. His personality conveys to us a sense of poise, self-control, understanding, tranquility. He creates an atmosphere of confidence. His very presence denotes strength, and it gives you a LIFT.

PRAYER BRINGS JOY

PRAYER is the key that unlocks the door to miracles in your life.

PRAYER is an ATTITUDE. An attitude that you must have that *"my Father knows what I have need of."*

PRAYER is a RELATIONSHIP. A close relationship—you with God. God is your source, your light, and is the Supreme Power of the Universe. *"In Him I live, move, and have my being."*

PRAYER must be powered by DESIRE, my desire for the best things in life—the God-like quality in self. The degree of your ATTITUDE plus RELATIONSHIP plus DESIRE is the power that can change your life. Miracles can happen if you make them happen.

The RESULT of your prayer depends upon the BELIEF that your heart exercises! Prayer is the key to Successful Living. Through prayer I find God and God finds me. PRAYER IS UNION WITH THE POWER BY WHICH WE LIVE. Prayer is the tie between the individual and the Great Spirit. It is the human soul searching for its relationship. Men cannot live greatly without it. God abides within my soul, *"the Kingdom of God is within."* He is my best friend.

I know of no really great man in history who has not been a man of prayer. The human side of life is as inseparably joined to prayer as it is to breathing. There is a Master-Mind back of the mystery of prayer Who has given all necessary instructions for its use.

If the work of God could be comprehended by reason it would be no longer wonderful. FAITH would have no merit if reason provided the proof. The results are the proof of faith.

LOYALTY IS AN ELEMENT OF HAPPINESS

LOYALTY IS RARE, IT IS ONLY PROVEN UNDER TEST.

If virtues could be graded, LOYALTY would stand near the top of the list. It is as priceless as it is rare. It creates a quiet confidence in the heart of any leader, and is the assurance of success in any enterprise.

Given LOYALTY, all things being equal, there can be no thought of faltering on the part of a leader. It is the sun that warms his darkest day and the strength of his life.

No leader, no matter how great or good or gifted, can accomplish the task to which he is assigned without the loyalty, cooperation and sacrificial devotion of those associated with him. We must labor together with the utmost of our ability.

Therefore your LOYALTY is one of the great contributing factors in the growth and prosperity of every worthwhile work. No organization is greater than the loyalty of the people it employs.

Abraham Lincoln admonished: *"I am not bound to win, but I am bound to be true. I am not bound to succeed, but I am bound to live by the light that I have. I must stand with anybody that stands right, stand with him while he is right, and part with him when he goes wrong."*

THE SUCCESSFUL MAN HAS LOYALTY!

HOW DOES ONE KNOW HIMSELF?

A few days ago a prominent businessman asked me, "How does one know himself?" This question took me by surprise, but it shouldn't have. Two thousand years ago Socrates said, "*Man, know thyself.*" This is one of the most important admonitions given to man. Sounds simple but how profound! Very few men know themselves. Everyman's heart cries out for a better life.

My answer was that man knows himself by the knowledge of and use of the laws of his own nature. The truth is that this is what determines the quality of his life. The forty-seven laws of man's nature are the essence of my latest book, *The Supreme Philosophy of Man*. To know and use these principles properly is the secret of noble living.

Man is a three-dimensional creature. To develop the whole man all three dimensions must be developed equally. Man's three major divine dimensions are his body (physical), his mind (mental), his spirit or soul (spiritual).

The business of every person is the continual development of himself physically, mentally, spiritually, throughout his entire lifetime. And also to realize that he has only a limited time to get the job done. Every thinking person should first realize who he is, what his true nature is, why he is here, and where he is going. Today the average man knows more about his automobile than he does about himself. WE HAVE LOST OUR CONCEPTION OF OUR NATURE WITH ITS DIVINE DIMENSIONS.

When you realize who you are—a god in your own right—and how wonderfully you are made, you do not merely exist, YOU LIVE! You know yourself when you realize: 1) No man can hurt you but yourself. 2) Your thoughts make or break you. 3) Everything depends on your attitude, not on things around you. 4) You must be useful or you will come unglued. These are just a few of the answers you will have when you "know yourself." Socrates admonished, "*Man know thyself.*" Get to know your qualities so as to enlarge them; and your failings, so as to reduce them. Seneca, the Latin philosopher and tutor of Nero, wrote, "*As long as you live, keep learning how to live.*"

Our world at present is full of problems: social, economic, political, racial and religious. These problems exist only because they are man's individual problems multiplied many times. BEHIND IT ALL LIES A LACK OF FULL KNOWLEDGE AND COMPLETE UNDERSTANDING OF THE SPIRITUAL LAWS AND PRINCIPLES THAT GOVERN THE HEARTS OF MEN.

Insist on remaining an individual and showing the world what YOU, as an unique entity, have to offer. We, within us, have assets and liabilities, and if we are willing to know ourselves a little better, then we will understand what our assets and liabilities are. Happiness and success do not just happen. They are the effect of what we are inside. Our happiness and our success is woven out of the fabric of our daily attitudes, thoughts, feelings, opinion, actions and reactions.

The opportunities for acquiring material wealth are greater now than ever before. In our eagerness to attain material things we tend to forget our own ideals and sometimes place too much emphasis on material gain. We do nevertheless come to the realization that there are other things which are even more important. This can be attributed to the average person's strong sense of values.

When I talk to college graduates I am amazed and astounded at how few know the laws of their own nature. THESE LAWS ARE THE ROOT CAUSE OF EVERYTHING THAT HAPPENS TO THEM, GOOD OR BAD—SUCCESS, RICHES, FRIENDSHIP, HAPPINESS—OR DISASTER. *Discovering man's nature is therefore the highest human enterprise . . . the greatest wisdom . . . the only path to the best life known.*

In these so-called days of enlightenment, very few people know or understand the laws of man's nature. Yet nature's laws are supreme. Education has failed to teach that every man is brought to true knowledge by the refinement and discipline of his own nature. Today some of the students even threaten the teachers. At one time education taught discipline. WITH THE TRUE KNOWLEDGE OF NATURE'S LAWS YOU HAVE THE BASIS FOR ALL REAL SUCCESS AND THE KEY TO WISDOM. THE KNOWHOW FOR BETTER LIVING. Unless one develops his spiritual qualities and has a gentle, humble heart, education per se can be a curse instead of a blessing. Without the spiritual development the educated will always exploit the ignorant.

Success in its fullest and happiest sense depends upon self-discovery. How well do we know ourselves and our capabilities? The best informed man is the one who *"Knows Himself."* Remember Socrates' famous phrase, *"The unexamined life is not worth living."* Make it thy business to know thyself, which is the most difficult business in the world.

Maturity, competence, peace of mind and happiness require a much fuller range of values, talents, and social skills than just academic excellence. TO BUILD A MAN IS LIFE'S GREATEST PROJECT . . . FOR EACH OF US.

How Does One Know Himself?

Man is born a long way from himself. It takes a long time to "Know Thyself," some never do. He needs to see the end (eternal life) toward which he moves. The immediate is so small it must be absorbed by the future. The measure of his strength must be revealed by a vision of his highest faculty, which is from the higher Divine Power of God. He must see the unseen, and work in the realm of the invisible (spiritual)! Happy is the man who learns that the present is but the challenge of his future. His FAITH in the Divine Power and future helps him to overcome situations. THIS IS THE BIG PICTURE—THE FAR LOOK—LIFE AT ITS BEST!

Many people have lost their conception of their divine dimension. The entire ministry of Jesus Christ was to get His people in good spiritual condition. When this is done, then the rest of life will look after itself, because you will find the major answers in your life when you *"Know Yourself."*

The greatest discovery anyone can make is to discover his true self, and develop the latent power that lies within. Discover the power of constructive thought, the value of a cheerful and wholesome attitude. Discover the unlimited inner power. Man has not even scratched the surface of his own nature, and the truth of his own existence.

We live in a day when so many are occupied with the "outer man" while the "inner man" perishes. The tendency today is to ignore man's inner nature and his eternal welfare, as if he did not have a spirit, a mind, or a soul.

Former President Harry S. Truman wrote: *"I fear we are much too much concerned with material things to remember that our real strength lies in spiritual values. I doubt whether there is in this troubled world a single problem that could not be solved if approached in the spirit of the Sermon on the Mount."*

I WONDER

Shall I ever live in a world:

Where every man will look every other man in the eyes and mean exactly what he says?

Where men will search for faults in themselves as diligently as they search for faults in others?

Where men have a greater sense of responsibility to God than to anyone or anything else?

Where those entrusted with confidence and responsibility will think of confidence and responsibility as sacred trusts?

Where even the great will not feel themselves above performing small duties with conscientious devotion?

Where everyone will mind his own business—

And give to others the same liberty they demand for themselves . . .

And enjoy seeing others enjoy what they do not enjoy . . .

And think the best even though they fear the worst?

Shall I ever live in such a world?

I WONDER!

IF YOU SEE SOMEONE

WITHOUT A SMILE

GIVE HIM YOURS.

GO INTO THE FIELDS

Professor Blaikie of Edinburgh used to tell his students: *"We shall never have another era of creative literature until our scholars become out-of-doors men."* He urged his students to *"take their books and go into the fields, and amid the solitudes, walk and reflect."*

Cities are NOT CONDUCIVE TO GREAT THOUGHTS. They do not, because they cannot, build great men. The country must produce great men, then send them to do missionary work in the cities.

Read the biographies of great men of all the centuries and be convinced. From Moses to the Christ, greatness has ever walked with God in the open. Jesus never entered a city, only when He had to.

His place of prayer was a mountain, and His favorite pulpit was a field. Beasts and birds, lilies and grasses, lakes and rivers, seeds and soil, clouds and rocks, were His texts, and from them He drew His illustrations to teach us essential truth.

The best of men need now and again to leave the lowlands where, all too often, our estimate of values becomes so confused that we sell the fine gold of worthwhile things to the junk man for scrap iron, and where, amid the confusion of tongues, we often utterly fail to interpret the language of the heart.

You HAVE to live in the city? Well, have a yard and a tree and there meditate and commune with Him who only can make a tree. Trees fascinate me. They speak a language I know and understand. Sprawled in the shade, I have listened to the music that dripped from their softly stirring leaves. Listen and watch the sparrows and mockingbirds, and they will teach you Happiness.

THE SIMPLE
HAPPY LIFE

Abraham Lincoln was a man who cut through all the smoke and baloney and got to the core quickly and briefly. You don't need to know ten million things, just know the one right thing. This is the secret of a farmer who has wisdom. The secret of anybody who really has wisdom. You don't need to know ten million things which are little things and all work against you. You must know certain things well. That is what I call ESSENTIAL KNOWLEDGE, meaning indispensable truth. *One can live and die very successfully without knowing plenty.*

This business that there are all these things in the world that can't be understood is a lot of baloney. Anything that can't be understood doesn't exist. And instead of being complex, sometimes it is in the simplicity that you understand them. Some people, including those in the government, would call this view simplistic because they have a word for everything. Consequently, they will confuse you with a hundred different issues.

All truth is simple. There are very simple principles to be used in our lives. It is man who complicates his own life. The minute everything sounds highly intellectual, man becomes confused. True, there are many mysteries, but this does not mean they are not a fact. *"We are losing our sense of leisure,"* says a contemporaneous poet-philosopher. Never were truer words spoken. In a frenzy we rush through the days and weeks, not living life, but consuming it.

Henry Thoreau was an advocate of the simple life, and an observer of nature. He resolved to try a great back-to-nature experiment and chose Walden Pond as an appropriate setting. He felt that the individual should go directly back to nature and find nature's ways and live according to them . . . experience the joy of living.

Grenville Kleiser wrote, "*Whether you are eighty or eighteen, let simplicity govern your life. Use and enjoy what you have. Be grateful for present blessings and opportunities. True happiness does not depend upon great material possessions, but emanates largely from a mental attitude of contentment, confidence, serenity, and beneficence. Simplicity of life tends always to happiness.*"

Thoreau admonished: "*Simplicity . . . simplicity . . . simplicity. I say, let your affairs be as two or three, and not a hundred or a thousand; instead of a million, count half a dozen and keep your accounts on your thumbnail.*"

Your life is what you make it. Your life can be simple if you will set it up with simplicity as a goal. It will take courage to cut away from the thousand and one hindrances that make life complex, but it can be done. Life becomes a mad scramble for gain and speed, at the expense of one's health and peace of mind. We must learn to simplify our lives.

Why not use the few years that we have to accomplish something in terms of ourselves rather than in terms of money or possessions or our dependencies? Why should we not try to unfold the latent potential of our own natures, develop our full potential? Why should we be surrounded by things that grow naturally, and then, in our own lives, grow as artificially as possible?

Thoreau was deeply suspicious of progress, as we call it. He saw in it almost nothing but complication rewarded by anxiety. Thoreau felt that we pay too high a price for the achievements which have so little essential merit in themselves.

"Life is not complex. We are complex. Life is simple, and the simple thing is the right thing," wrote Oscar Wilde.

Some way there should be a detachment in which the person is able to extricate himself from THE COMPLICATIONS OF HIS OWN AMBITIONS. In substance, of what use is ambition in a world in which all things in the end come to disillusion? The ambitious man is rewarded with a few years of success, and after these years he departs, and whether he succeeds or does not succeed is of no lasting significance.

It is also obvious that many of our most tragic situations arise from this desperate determination to attain WEALTH, FAME or a STATUS of some kind.

Simplicity has often been called the mark of true greatness. SIMPLICITY IS THE BADGE OF DISTINCTION. The more simply you live, the more secure is your future; you are less at the mercy of surprises and reverses. SIMPLICITY OF LIFE TENDS ALWAYS TO HAPPINESS. Ask yourself: Why should I do this? Is this necessary? The truly wise are always simple. All great things are simple. Keep it simple and it will be understood.

SIMPLIFY your life by pursuing your most important priorities first. One way is to be selective in accepting invitations or making commitments that take your time and energy. Associate with people where you INVEST your time—don't just SPEND your time.

The wise man will ever seek to simplify his life. The greatest truths are the simplest and so are the greatest men. We should save ourselves from hopeless involvement in our own ambitions and desires. We should evaluate our possessions and activities, and eliminate those which have no essential value. There are many things we can simplify, if we so desire. *Take inventory of your life to see what happened. Man must wake up and realize there is more to life than scientific progress, and a decay of the natural elements of happy living.*

We are all driving along toward the achievement of our own inner inordinate desires; yet when we attain those desires we are not happy. The more progressive we become, the more miserable we are, and the greater our advantages, the heavier our responsibilities. The person, as a natural creature living in a natural world, has almost no opportunity to exist. He has surrounded himself with an artificial atmosphere, he has created a society for himself, he has defined his own creation, and assumes that normalcy is to agree with the common attitudes, most of which may be wrong.

SUCCESS

To get PROFIT without RISK
   . . . EXPERIENCE without DANGER
     . . . and REWARD without WORK
       . . . Is as IMPOSSIBLE as it is
         . . . TO LIVE WITHOUT BEING BORN.

—Alfred Armand Montapert,
PERSONAL PLANNING MANUAL

TODAY'S INVESTMENT—
TOMORROW'S DIVIDEND

The United States of America is doomed to be captured. An army will march throughout the length and breadth of our great land. Its soldiers will march into the White House and there place their own president. They will elect their own Congress and appoint their own judiciary. They will commandeer all our resources. They will take over our churches and preach what they will. They will appropriate our schools and teach what they will.

This vast army is on the march—it is our YOUTH! They are being reared in our homes, educated in our schools, and getting their conceptions of God and spiritual values in our churches. What they will be when they take over depends upon us. We are the reason for the delinquency which we decry so loudly.

It was Goethe who said, *"The future of any nation is determined by the opinions of its youth under twenty-five years of age."* And mothers, good or bad, pretty largely shape these opinions.

The influence of good mothers upon our national life can scarcely be overestimated. THE HOME IS OUR GREATEST INSTITUTION. Our libraries are full of histories of war, commerce, literature, and finance, but strangely enough no writer has ever seen fit to write a history of the home and its influence upon the life of a nation.

If Fisk and Bryce have written the history of our laws and institutions, it remains for serious students to trace these laws and institutions back to the love and instruction and forethought of great, good women. If *"in the shadows standeth God,"* just as surely behind the scenes has stood a good mother molding, inspiring, and directing every great man who has wrought mightily for national greatness and security.

Napoleon once said, *"The future of France is its homes."* Time proved his prediction true. Until her homes began to deteriorate France was invincible. A Roman historian says, *"The Roman Empire began its decline when Roman homes declined."*

There never was a great man who did not have a great mother. If you doubt this statement, try to find a great man or great woman who was not helped and inspired to greatness by a noble mother. At the mother's knee, around the home fireside, the foundations of life are laid. Great persons are great because of good, strong foundations on which they were able to build a character.

While some are shouting they need this and that, the crying need of the hour—if there is to be any future—is GODLY MOTHERS AND PRAYERFUL GOD-FEARING FATHERS. Without doubt, a man mothered by a godly woman will inherit a worthy theme for living, and become the expression of a worthy sentiment. He will inherit a robust fury against wrong and injustice, persistence in a righteous cause, and patient devotion to high ideals. HE WILL CARRY WITH HIM TO HIS LATEST BREATH, THE ENVIRONMENT THAT ONLY A GOOD MOTHER CAN WILL TO AN INTELLIGENT DEVOTED SON OR DAUGHTER— and amid the shadows of a fading day, they will thank God that they were born of a good mother and inherited the riches of her heart. NOBLE PARENTS HAVE NOBLE CHILDREN.

HAPPINESS IS A BROOK

Some find in the ocean that indefinable something that answers a mood and inspires a dream. The vast expanse of restless water, with its eternal power washing up in broken boom along a ragged shoreline, seems to blend its deep bass with the haunting minor music of a pensive mood, and weave itself into a melody that speaks the language of other worlds.

But give me a *brook*. The ocean is too remote. The brook is intimate. Yesterday I sat for an hour or two beside the singing, restful flow of one. Like a shaft of sunlight it came out of a shadowy canyon and went searching its way to the valley below.

It set me dreaming . . . and wondering. I wondered where it took its rise. I wondered how many other little streams had come out of their hiding to join its flow. I wondered where its gathered waters would mingle themselves with other waters, and finally merge their music into the vast symphony of still mightier music.

And then I mused: How like life. It too takes its rise in mystery and, like the little brook, begins its meandering journey down the canyon that we call years . . . sometimes through sunny places, sometimes through shadowy, treacherous places . . . but ever going on intent to reach some goal.

If, thought I, my life, like the brook, can make some music, give some pleasure to others, water some barren places, and finally merge into the vast, eternal music of the purpose of God, I too shall have filled an exalted mission.

THE COUNTRY IS A HAPPY PLACE

So you're going to the city to see the sights? Well, when you've seen the city, you haven't seen anything. If you would see the sights, go to the hills where Spring is clothing the trees with new, soft green, and painting sunsets gold and crimson. Stand awhile and listen to a mocking bird fill the valley with music that flows like molten silver, and feel the wind in your face.

Watch the miracle of blooming jonquils and breathe the fragrance of wild lilacs. Wait until the hills silhouette themselves against the sky where the sunset burns out like the glow of dying embers and the little voices come in from far and near. There, my friend, you will see and feel and hear God.

Cowper wrote, *"God made the country and man made the town."* A country life gives a man greater health and more perfect enjoyment of himself than any other way of life. Amos B. Alcott admonished, *"I consider it the best part of an education to have been born and brought up in the country."* Life in the country teaches one that the really stimulating things are the quiet, natural things, and the really wearisome things are the noisy, unnatural things.

Sixty percent of your ENERGY comes from the air you breathe, the other forty percent from the food you eat. Why does a man feel good when he spends some time in the country, at the seashore, or the mountains, or the desert? It is because he is in his natural environment, he is away from the synthetic world. Nothing more surely ranks a man as his love for nature or lack of it. *That yesteryear that sired great men was the era of farms, small villages and broad vistas of countryside . . . of trees and birds and brooks and rivers and lakes.*

HAPPINESS DEPENDS ON PLANNED ACTION

If the architect must have his plans and the construction engineer must have his blueprints to build the building, how MUCH MORE do we need a set of PLANS to build happy lives.

The builder of a good life MUST have his plans for the years ahead. *The greatest responsibility given to each one of us is to develop ourselves.* One of the most important attributes for every person to develop and acquire is Happiness.

One way to help accomplish this is to apply the principles of good planning. Plan and improve each of the different departments of your life: Financial—Personal—Business—Health—Mental—Family and Home—Travel and Culture—Social—Spiritual—Retirement.

PLANNING IS A MUST in order to build a good life. Write down all the PLANS—OBJECTIVES—GOALS you want to accomplish in the next five years. Keep adding to these. Then break them down into steps. This is what makes it easier. Be flexible in your planning. It is dangerous to base your actions on the assumption that everything is going to continue as it is.

A building is built brick by brick. A painting is achieved stroke by stroke. A book is written word by word. Success is acquired step by step, step by step, STEP BY STEP. There is no other way.

Happiness Depends On Planned Action

Life is like a grand staircase—some people are going up and some people are going down. *The direction of your life, whether you go up or down, will depend on the PLANS you make.*

A great many people spend more time planning a vacation than they do their life. When you plan a trip, the first thing you do is to get a road map. Your written plans are practical steps to help your efforts to grow, to develop your hidden talents, to change your life in a meaningful and beneficial direction. To maximize your own chances of success. Living Happily is a lifetime job.

You are the architect and builder of your own HAPPINESS—LIFE—FORTUNE—DESTINY. You had better live your best, think your best, and do your best TODAY, for today will soon be tomorrow and tomorrow will soon be forever.

This message can be wrapped up in two words: MAKE PLANS!

Alexis Carrel writes, *"The most effective way to live reasonably is every morning to make a plan of one's day, and every night to examine the results obtained."*

MOTIVATION

MOVE OUT, MAN! LIFE IS FLEETING BY.

DO SOMETHING WORTHWHILE, BEFORE YOU DIE.

LEAVE BEHIND A WORK SUBLIME.

THAT WILL OUTLIVE YOU, AND TIME.

—*Alfred Armand Montapert,*
PERSONAL PLANNING MANUAL

MAN'S MOST HAPPY GOAL

Man's most happy goal is his spiritual development. Be glad that you have searched for TRUTH early and late. TRUTH is all we shall have when the sun sets on our years. Without the TRUTH we shall die bankrupt.

THIS IS THE BIG PICTURE IN OUR LIFE. The sad thing is only few realize it. What truths have we learned during our lifetime? Great truths are timeless. In the long run, digging for truth has always proved not only more interesting but more profitable than digging for gold. Light is light, though the blind man does not see it. Jesus said, *"Ye shall know the truth and the truth shall set you free."*

"There is a Higher Power that is the source of everything good . . . GOD." Therefore, we must develop our spiritual dimension for that is the unseen where we gather our power to overcome and enjoy the present . . . to give us hope for the future . . . to satisfy the infinite nature of the you of you. We look to the inexhaustible God, only HE can satisfy our soul.

The truth taught by Jesus Christ is the right way to live. He is God's revelation of how life MUST be lived to be lived at its best. To misunderstand, or fail to grasp this truth, is to miss the whole purpose of God's revelation of Himself in Jesus Christ. To accept and believe it is at once to give us an intelligent conception of the whole scheme of things called LIFE. You will find His amazing words true. *"I am the WAY, the TRUTH and the LIFE. I am come that they might HAVE LIFE."* TRUTH IS ETERNAL!

GOOD PHILOSOPHY FOR HAPPINESS

Do the BEST you can EACH DAY.

THINK and PLAN first, then DO secondly, then ENJOY the FRUITS of your labor.

Do not waste TIME, for time is the RAW MATERIAL OF LIFE.

Live CONSTRUCTIVELY and live OPTIMISTICALLY.

LIVE to ENJOY the money you make.

Abide by the GOLDEN RULE. (Matthew 7:12) Abide by the SERMON ON THE MOUNT. (Matthew 5, 6, 7)

Nothing in life is STATIC; one must LEARN to make adjustments.

Never admit defeat. LIVE CONFIDENTLY.

Always look for the GOOD in others; no one is perfect.

Think WELL of yourself, as the world takes you at your own estimate.

Beware of THIRST for the wrong kind of pleasures; cut off wrong pleasures and replace with the REAL PLEASURES of life.

UNDERSTAND the Law of CAUSE and EFFECT. I will suffer if I violate it. It becomes my greatest friend if I understand it.

Every EXCESS has its EFFECT, its AFTERMATH, its HANGOVER. EVERYTHING that exceeds the bounds of MODERATION has an UNSTABLE FOUNDATION.

HAPPINESS DEPENDS NOT ON THINGS around me, but on my ATTITUDE. Everything in my life will depend on my ATTITUDE.

You serve GOD best by serving your fellowman.

THE SCHOOL OF LIFE

Life has been likened to a school. All things considered, it is a good simile.

The school bell rings at birth. It need never be rung again. School is never out. Nor are there any vacations or holidays. The curriculum is exacting. The lessons are hard. The course is prescribed. There are no elective subjects. Professor Time plays no favorites. The Superintendent is concerned only with ETERNAL VALUES. He is determined that all shall graduate with honors.

While we may not elect a course in the School of Life, we may specialize in certain subjects. I have chosen for myself certain subjects in which you may be interested, also.

I want to know:

How to keep the symphony of my life in tune with the Infinite.

How to gain the wisdom to order my life in such a way as to achieve my own highest good while keeping due regard for the opinions, rights, and privacies of others.

How to obtain the highest legitimate reward for myself, without robbing others by failing to always give value received.

How to capitalize on my own disappointments and weaknesses so that I shall be able to enrich others with understanding, encouragement, and helpfulness.

How, when wounded in life's battle, to draw the water of hope and courage from the deep wells of quiet meditation and prayer, and return to the conflict undaunted and unafraid.

How to keep a due appreciation of myself, my abilities, and whatever of value I may have accomplished without becoming egotistical, arrogant, and boastful—knowing that self-depreciation is a cardinal sin and egotism is a cancerous growth.

How to gracefully say, "I do not know," rather than attempt to bluff in the name of wisdom, and by so doing reveal my ignorance the more clearly to those who do know; and thus become an object of pity and contempt when I might have kept their respect and confidence by being honest.

How to be a happy person and to take charge of my life, not the whole world.

How to use several languages when the occasion required it, but how to keep silent in all several languages most of the time.

How to occasionally let others have the last word even though I know they are wrong.

How to wear a victor's laurel gracefully, and how to accept defeat just as gracefully.

How to acquire wisdom and yet keep my place in the Kingdom of God with the faith and simplicity of a little child.

And finally, how to keep constantly before me the truth that God's *"well done"* is more important than the passing approbation of men who themselves have never known the true meaning of life.

These are the subjects in which I am most interested, and which I conceive to be of paramount importance.

This book, too, can be likened to a series of practical lessons in successful living for the school of life. Its purpose is to help people to help themselves . . . to offer realistic answers to man's basic problems . . . to increase the value and joy of human life and decrease the amount of suffering . . . to ease man's mind and *bring happiness into his heart*.

Let shallow minds reject and ridicule as they may, the fact remains that God's truth is at the center of all education in living, for there is no explanation of the universe, nor of man, apart from the creative genius of God.

LIFE is a series of accomplishments and adventures. When you have reached one goal or adventure it loses its drive. But there are more goals ahead. One never really runs out of goals and adventures. This is called GROWTH, to LEARN, to GROW, to BECOME. The object of all learning is so that you can use it in the future. It is only by LEARNING HOW TO THINK and by learning how to sift out things worth thinking about that you can put yourself in the best position for enjoying a happy life.

No man ever graduates from the School of Life. He is a student to the end, and in his last breath he may still learn. All life is a process of learning. Step #1 is to LEARN, Step #2 is to APPLY what is learned. Know how to USE this learning. Step #3 is ENJOYING what you have done, getting satisfaction out of a job well done . . . being HAPPY. Even though the world is full of suffering and strife, you can BECOME a solid person of STERLING CHARACTER and WORTH, and have HAPPINESS in your heart.

SUMMARY

It has been our purpose to awaken your interest in the most rewarding of all arts, the ART OF BEING HAPPY, and to show the way to happiness and to stimulate and encourage the reader to see and do for himself.

Men have achieved happiness through seemingly different ways. This little book by no means exhausts all the elements of happiness, but it will provide you with an excellent foundation for Happiness and Contentment.

The time has come for the reshaping of our ideas of goodness, longing, sorrow, as well as of happiness. Let us achieve the calmness of the soul and joys of living. THE WHOLE OF LIFE AND HAPPINESS IS NOTHING BUT A CONTINUOUS EDUCATION OF ONESELF BY ONESELF. HAPPINESS IS NOT A GIFT, IT IS AN ACHIEVEMENT.

"Men can alter their lives by altering their attitudes," said William James. Joy depends not on things around us, but on our attitude. Everything in our lives depends upon our attitude. It's a never ending job to develop the positive qualities that lead to success, and weed out the negative traits, worry, fear, hate, envy, that prevent us from attaining real happiness, security and the joy of accomplishment.

If modern man were more concerned with what he IS, and less dominated by what he HAS, his fears would diminish. Little by little, man becomes aware that his own code of conduct is the basis of his own security. REAL SECURITY IS HAVING A SENSE OF GOD. The accomplishment of the greatest good is the fundamental purpose of life. A PERSON CAN NO MORE BUILD A LIFE WITHOUT SOLID BELIEFS AND IDEALS THAN HE CAN BUILD A BUILDING WITHOUT A SOLID FOUNDATION.

Happiness is VICTORY over life's troubles.
Happiness in the home is the spring of life.
Happiness is found in good books.
Happiness is seen in the beauty of nature.
Happiness is found in work.
Happiness is found in helping others.
Happiness is found in good music and art.
Happiness is found in travel, companionship.
Happiness is lost in hurry—worry—and debt.
Happiness and contentment are found in hope.
Happiness is knowing "God cares for me."

Charles (Tremendous) Jones, one of the greatest speakers in the world, admonishes: "Every day I expect lots of problems and I thrive on them. If something good does come along or happens, I don't let it bother me—I'll manage to work it in somehow!"

Summing up, therefore, we may define the Happy Life as the life in which one seeks maximum personal development in every direction, maintaining true balance between Body, Mind, Spirit. It is what YOU BECOME, what YOU ARE, not the vast knowledge or money you may have.

It took a lifetime of experience in the arena of the business world to write this essay on HAPPINESS. For years I was engaged in the day-to-day arena of economic survival. My ideas were tested constantly by the very highest and most brutal standards . . . those of the market place. If you master the essence of this book you will receive the most rewarding of all human achievements, THE ART OF HAPPINESS AND JOY!

We marvel when we think of the wealth of elements which make up the Way to Happiness. Regardless of how many degrees you have, you are not truly educated until you have mastered the ESSENCE of what we have written. Give happiness to others . . . and you will find it in yourself.

MAKE every day a happy day! The more we reflect, the more we perceive that happiness dwells within us. Through a regrettable lack of comprehension, we wear out our lives seeking it elsewhere.

The end of all learning is that the human heart shall find peace in communion with its Creator, and be able to express this peace through thought, emotion, and conduct. Your FAITH in God is your FORTUNE.

Today, man's relationship with God is wrong. When man really sees that he just cannot deal with evil and selfishness in human hearts, he will wake up to find what has really wrecked all his schemes.

You have FREE CHOICE, it is for you to choose which you will make your very own. We cannot expect to be happy if we do not lead pure, clean, and useful lives.

HAPPINESS

The Eternal Quest of Mankind Depends Upon . . . . .

. . . THE CHARACTER OF YOUR THOUGHTS.
. . . SOME VOCATION WHICH SATISFIES THE SOUL.
. . . THE ABILITY TO GIVE VALUE TO YOUR EXISTENCE.

FOR HAPPINESS DEPENDS UPON WHAT LIES BETWEEN THE SOLES OF YOUR FEET AND THE CROWN OF YOUR HEAD.

WE MUST SEARCH FOR HAPPINESS IN WHAT WE ARE, RATHER THAN IN WHAT WE HAVE. There is no genuine happiness without God. When we come to know God and experience the truth, He is the Life and Life Eternal. When we live in His will and His way, we will know divine happiness and joy. This is the only way to reach your FULL POTENTIAL. HAPPY IS THE MAN WHO FIRST KNOWS WHAT HAPPINESS IS . . . WHO THEN ACCEPTS NO SUBSTITUTE.

The world measures success and happiness in terms of money and power. Jesus came to make people happy, and measured success in terms of happiness, inner peace, love and joy, and the capacity NOT to dominate others, but to serve them and make them happy. In accepting Jesus Christ as our Saviour we will have peace and joy and happiness that is beyond words to express. Tap into the awesome power of God . . . a quality of life that the world knows nothing about.

And so, dear reader, we come to the end of our little journey through this book together. May God open the windows of heaven upon you and pour out His blessings, and fill your life with happiness and joy!

ALWAYS REMEMBER THE MOST IMPORTANT PRODUCT OF YOUR LIFE IS HAPPINESS AND JOY . . . WHICH IS THE BY-PRODUCT OF FAITH, HOPE AND LOVE.

I dedicate this book to my wife, Evelyn, who has brought happiness, joy, love and gladness into my life.

I am the happiest man I know!

—Alfred Armand Montapert